TRADITIONAL HOME

June/July 2001

CLASSIC DECORATING WITH A TWIST

BACKYARD STORYBOOK GARDEN

GIRLFRIENDS FOR THE WEEKEND

BIG ON SMALL

MORE STYLE AND COMFORT IN LESS SPACE

The new Chevy™ Tahoe® has an optional third-row seat that can go pretty much anywhere. Each half s

when you aren't carrying nine people, each half flips and folds out of the way for extra cargo

STINE RIVERS, THE BREATHTAKING VISTAS,
LIT THIRD-ROW SEAT.

*Versus 1999 model. ©2000 GM Corp. Buckle up, America!

ns just over 40 pounds, has handles and is on rollers, so it's easy to take out or put back in. And

new Chevy Tahoe. It's nowhere near anything. Call 800-950-2438 or visit chevrolet.com

TAHOE

LIKE A ROCK

A R D T

Viking products are marketed under the Ultraline™ brand name in Canada.

VIKING *christens its new* FLE

The Viking Designer Series sets sail with an entirely new look for professional performance.

Clean lines and sweeping curves make for a striking appearance. While high-powered

features ensure smooth sailing through even the most daring gourmet dishes.

The complete line is now docked at your nearest Viking dealer.

VIKING®
DESIGNER SERIES

www.vikingrange.com 1-888-845-4641

A.

1. A striking resemblance, but guess again.
2. Pergo Select, the crème de la crème de la laminate.
3. As many design ideas as you've got rooms, and then some.
4. At authorized Pergo dealers–probably right in your neighborhood.
5. LusterGard™ Plus. Our secret recipe for scratch protection.
6. Nope, no other brand has it.
7. The nice, comforting effect of a 25-year Wall-To-Wall Warranty.
8. Samples of the flooring are a good start. Order them at www.pergo.com.
9. A free idea book available on-line or at 1-800-33-PERGO.
10. Some of them may be edible, but we'll just stick with arugula and lettuce.

PERGO®

The revolutionary laminate floor from Sweden.

IN A COUNTRY WHERE SIZE COUNTS, SMALL IS FINALLY GETTING some well-deserved respect. While "McMansions"—those monstrous houses that literally bulge from their lots—are still being built in many parts of the country, there are exceptions to the bigger-is-better rule: Houses and apartments chosen because they're on the slim side. Spaces that are extraordinary because their small size inspires innovative design.

For example, when *Traditional Home*'s architecture and art editor Eliot Nusbaum showed me photos of the Evanston, Illinois, home of interior designer Sheila Barron, we both knew we were looking at a gold mine. Beautiful, elegant, functional—the Georgian-style house had it all, except for an expansive floor plan. The 2,000-square-foot house is modest by almost any standard, but Sheila made the petite two-story structure live graciously with the inclusion of interior columns and deep moldings, a calming ochre-and-cream palette, and fine touches of gilt, crystal, and polished woods. (See our story on pages 123–131.)

Another master at making the most of small spaces is Dixie Allen, whose Washington, D.C., home we feature on pages 28–36. Only 20 feet wide, the Federal-style row house is the perfect personal expression of Dixie's professional talents. Her business creates order and organization for homeowners and businesses alike—without losing sight of the need for style and comfort. One look at Dixie's home, and you'll be impressed by how beautiful and well-appointed small spaces can be.

While we might not all live in small homes, the space-transforming savvy of Sheila and the organizational wizardry of Dixie can motivate us to make more of the rooms we do have. Take the formal dining and living rooms at our house, for instance. While the traditionalist in me loves the idea of both rooms being beautifully pristine in their semiformal attire, the realist in me knows better. For all practical purposes, the living room is a music room—with a grand piano, violin, and string bass in residence. And the dining room is a project room; school-assignment models of a lighthouse and a Southern plantation are our current "centerpieces."

To improve the everyday usability of both rooms, I'm thinking of scrambling our existing furniture. The living room settee—newly slipcovered and outfitted with plump seat cushions—would be moved to the dining room. I'd place it against a wall with high-set windows, then snuggle the table up to it. The offset furniture arrangement would instantly create a more easygoing atmosphere and provide a comfortable, well-lit spot for the next projects our kids undertake. As for the living room, I envision a hiatus for the cocktail table and the addition of mates for the tufted club chair and ottoman that are already in place. That way, we'd have a cozy listening spot for two with a nice view of our front yard. When you have budding musicians to listen to, it's best to keep it simple.

Perhaps that's the reason why smart, small spaces are so inspirational. They do what big rooms do, without the fuss.

> ## IN LIVING QUARTERS, SMALL IS FINALLY GETTING SOME WELL-DESERVED RESPECT.

Karol DeWulf Nickell
Editor in Chief

Have a decorating question you'd like *Traditional Home* to answer? E-mail us at **traditionalhome@mdp.com**.

For more information, see the Reader's Resource on page 188.

BAKER

FURNITURE

BAKER. MOMENTS OF LIFE, AMONG THINGS OF BEAUTY.

TRADITIONAL HOME

123 COVER STORY

CONTENTS

VOLUME XII ISSUE III

154

168

24

Continued on page 12

COVER PHOTOGRAPH: GORDON BEALL

SCHUMACHER.

CONTENTS

142

52

177

164

62

Traditional Home®, June/July 2001 issue. *Traditional Home* is published by the Publishing Group of Meredith Corp., 1716 Locust St., Des Moines, IA 50309-3023. © COPYRIGHT MEREDITH CORPORATION 2001. ALL RIGHTS RESERVED. PRINTED IN U.S.A

JENN-AIR

©2003 jennair

Of course it's a downdraft. Why do you ask?

ATTRACTION

Experience the remarkable attraction of Jenn-Air. For decades, we've been perfecting

downdraft ventilation to beautifully clear the air without an overhead hood.

Our exclusive new range also features a high-performance, dual-speed convection

oven and a stunning, frameless glass cooktop. For information, visit jennair.com

or call 1-800-Jenn-Air. And feel the attraction of downdraft for yourself.

JENN-AIR

TRADITIONAL HOME.

Karol DeWulf Nickell
Editor in Chief

Jim Darilek	**Michael Diver**
Art Director	Managing Editor

Interior Design	Deborah Morant, Senior Editor
	Pamela J. Wilson, Editor
	Krissa Rossbund, Assistant Editor
Gardens	Elvin McDonald, Senior Staff Editor
Architecture and Art	Eliot Nusbaum, Senior Editor
Food and Entertaining	Carroll Stoner, Editor
Features and Antiques	Doris Athineos, Editor
Projects	Robert Young, Editor
Consumer Events	Jenny Bradley, Editor
Graphic Design	Dana Thompson, Associate Art Director
	Kristin Cleveland, Associate Art Director
Copy and Production	C. R. Mitchell, Copy Chief/Production Editor
Assistants	Anna Gosch, Administrative Assistant
	Jennifer Highland, Departmental Assistant
	Paul Pruangkarn, New York Editorial Assistant
Contributors	Rick Tramonto and Gale Gand, Contributing Chefs
	Ben and Karen Barker, Larry Forgione, Emeril Lagasse, Keith Luce, Alice Waters, Consulting Chefs
	Steed Hale, New York Editor

REGIONAL EDITORS

ATLANTA Lynn McGill	**CHICAGO** Elaine Markoutsas	**MINNEAPOLIS** Lisa Cicotte	**ST. LOUIS** Mary Anne Thomson
BALTIMORE Eileen Deymier	**DALLAS** Mary Baskin Amy Muzzy Malin	**NEW YORK** Bonnie Maharam	**SAN DIEGO** Andrea Caughey
BOSTON Estelle Bond Guralnick	**DES MOINES** Deb Riha	**NORTHBROOK, IL** Sally Mauer Hilary Rose	**SAN FRANCISCO** Helen Heitkamp Carla Breer Howard
BOULDER, CO Mindy Pantiel	**HOUSTON** Joetta Moulden	**PORTLAND, OR** Catherine A. Bradley Barbara Mundall	**SEATTLE** Trish Maharam
CHARLESTON, SC Lynn McBride	**INDIANAPOLIS** Betsy Harris		**TULSA** Nancy E. Ingram

Test Kitchen Director Lynn Blanchard
Photo Studio Manager Jeff Anderson

Editorial offices: Address letters and questions to The Editor, Traditional Home, 1716 Locust St., Des Moines, IA 50309-3023; fax 515/284-2083; e-mail us at traditionalhome@mdp.com

Customer Service Information: For service on your magazine subscription, including change of address, write to Traditional Home Customer Service, P.O. Box 37275, Boone, IA 50037-0275. Please enclose your address label from a recent issue. Or phone toll-free 800/374-8791.

May cause
excessive lingering.

Put Corian® solid surfaces in your kitchen and guests may never want to leave. Given its incredible warmth and inviting beauty, you can hardly blame them. For inspiration, visit us at corian.com or call 800-4CORIAN.

CORIAN
SOLID SURFACES
DUPONT

Corian® is a DuPont registered trademark. Only DuPont makes Corian?

To the naked eye,
all window glass
looks the same.
It's the naked body
that notices the
difference.

No matter what it's like outside, you should feel comfortable inside. So we make sure our window glass is as efficient as possible. It's all part of a uniquely Andersen philosophy of building, backing and servicing windows.

We call it the Perma-Shield® System. It includes

Clear Pine Interiors

The Perma-Shield System

Clad Wood Exteriors

unwavering attention to the details. Like our High-Performance™ insulated glass, with Low E² technology and the industry's best weatherstripping. In winter's icy grip or summer's smothering heat, you'll feel the difference.

Especially if all you're wearing is your birthday suit.

To learn more, call 1-800-426-4261, ext.3898

Worryproof. Timeproof.

Andersen Windows®.

www.andersenwindows.com

Andersen AW Windows·Patio Doors®

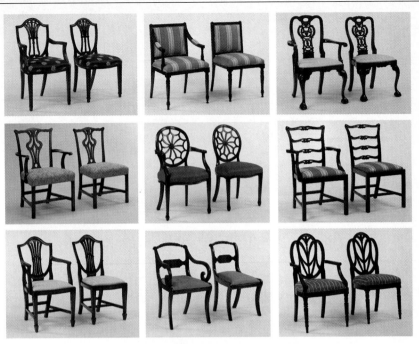

"Decisions, decisions, decisions."

JOHN EHRLICH

THE FEDERALIST presents the finest of classic chair designs. Sheraton, Adams, Hepplewhite, Chippendale and more. Each is made by hand using 18th century techniques. As always, THE FEDERALIST considers every detail to create furniture you will always cherish. Please call for our color brochures.

THE FEDERALIST®

We offer the finest hand made 18th century reproductions, including a wide range of furniture and decorative accessories.
369 Greenwich Ave. Greenwich, Ct. 06830 (203)625-4727 Fax (203)629-8775 Mon-Sat 10-6 Sun 12-5
Mail and telephone orders are accepted and we can ship anywhere in the world.

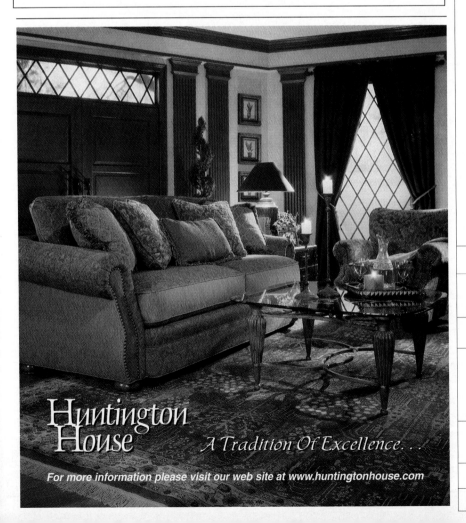

Huntington House

A Tradition Of Excellence...

For more information please visit our web site at www.huntingtonhouse.com

TRADITIONAL HOME.

Wilkie F. Bushby
Publisher

Pamela K. Daniels
Advertising Director

Christina M. Frohock
Director of Marketing and
Sales Promotion

NEW YORK
125 Park Ave., New York, NY 10017-5529
212/557-6600; Fax 212/551-6914
Sales Development Manager Katie J. Cohen
Account Managers
Kristina Carrington • Liana Johnson
W. Keven Weeks • Mandi Wyler
Marketing Director Renee M. Zuckerman
Events/Marketing Manager Susan Blackwood
Merchandising/Marketing Manager Shirley Young
Marketing Research Manager Irene Ochs-Lilien
Direct Response Advertising Director Patti Follo
ATLANTA
Brown & Company, 1055 Canton St., Suite 220,
Marietta, GA 30062; 770/998-2889; Fax 770/552-8250
Account Managers Byron Brown • Suzanne Cooper
CHICAGO
333 N. Michigan Ave., Chicago, IL 60601
312/580-1619; Fax 312/853-1224
Midwest Manager Denise Paull
Account Manager Lynn Caldwell
DETROIT
Maiorana & Partners, Ltd.
418 W. Fifth St., Suite C, Royal Oak, MI 48067
248/546-2222; Fax 248/546-0019
Account Managers
Colleen Maiorana • Laura Crouse
LOS ANGELES
11766 Wilshire Blvd., Suite 260, Los Angeles, CA 90025
310/479-0033; Fax 310/479-0713
West Coast Manager Brooke Fraser Bohm
SAN FRANCISCO
Demouth Associates, 6170 Mazuela Dr.,
Oakland, CA 94611; 510/339-2281; Fax 510/339-2283
Account Manager Mary Demouth
CANADA
Dodd Media Sales, 3121 Theatre Rd. N., RR4,
Cobourg, Ontario, Canada K9A 4J7
905/885-0664; Fax 905/885-0665
Account Manager Lori Dodd
LONDON
Durham House, Durham Place
London, England SW3 4ET 011-44-207-352-6121
Account Manager Lawrence Kane
ITALY
Wallace & Aprile Media, Inc.
Via Leon Battista Alberti, 5 20149 Milan
011-39-02-3361-4113

Advertising Services Manager
Karrie Nelson 515/284-3827

Circulation Director Jon Macarthy
Newsstand Director Terry Unsworth
Director of Operations Joanne Williams
Product Manager Dawn Drotzmann

Joe Lagani
Vice President/Publishing Director

MEREDITH PUBLISHING GROUP
Stephen M. Lacy, President
Jerry Kaplan, Magazine Group President; Michael Brownstein,
Group Sales; Ellen de Lathouder, Creative Services;
Bruce Heston, Manufacturing; Karla Jeffries, Circulation and
Consumer Marketing; Dean Pieters, Operations;
Max Runciman, Finance and Administration

Meredith
CORPORATION

WILLIAM T. KERR
Chairman and Chief Executive Officer

E. T. MEREDITH III, Chairman of the Executive Committee

Designed to keep you sound asleep and wide awake.

Sleeping well keeps you energized throughout the day. Orthopedic surgeons know this. And more of them sleep on a Sealy Posturepedic than on any other mattress. So why not enjoy the same deep sleep the back doctors get? After all, the day really begins the moment you fall asleep.

Sealy Posturepedic
We support you night and day.™

OUR READERS WRITE

Cuss Control

I don't listen to talk shows, and I buy only books I can afford (exclusively thrift-store!) So finding your article in *Traditional Home* magazine yesterday was surprising and refreshing. Hooray!

I'm just about to be a grandma, but decades ago, when I was a sweet young thing, decided that profanity didn't fit the kind of person I wanted to be. And for years, I really thought I was the only one who didn't cuss and didn't like others to! (My exclamation of choice was "Rats!"—which got big laughs in college.)

It has helped to have the support of a faith—though it came later—that reiterates that what comes out of one's mouth is significant . . . although other people tend to respond, "Aw, you don't swear just because you're so @!&%° religious!"

I do hope you have success in convincing at least a percentage of society that there are better, "cooler" things to do with one's mouth and one's mind. More power to you

Mary Lichlyt
via e-m

Continuing Tradition

I have just finished cataloging every issue of *Traditional Home* since February 1991, an I would like to thank you for being a constant source of pleasure and inspiration to me The magazine is evolving all the time while walking the fine line between maintaining the traditional look and accommodating new ideas, products, and tastes. There are so many things I love about *Traditional Home*—articles on furniture styles, antiques, and beautiful gardens and the homes they accompany. And my all-time favorite interior designer is Charles Faudree of Tulsa, Oklahoma.

Thanks again for continuing to produce such a fabulous publication.

Janet Stro
Woodlawn, Onta

Fortuny Remembered

Your article on Fortuny fabrics brought back wonderful memories of a dinner party I attended at Count Fortuny's palazzo many, many years ago. It was on one of the island with his factory next door. Of course, his home was exquisitely furnished, and the walls were completely covered in his creations.

I recall a magnificent micropleated silk he made that could be rolled up or folded fo packing without ever being wrinkled. I remember this fabric being worn by society ladies in the 1940s. It is said that when Mr. Fortuny died, the entire process of his fabrics died with him.

Thank you so much for this wonderful trip down memory lane.

Carmen Robins
Asheville, North Caroll

Learning to Mix Styles

I'd like to thank *Traditional Home* for providing such a great resource for fabulous ideas and beautiful photographs. Although I tend to like more casual furnishings, your magazine has taught me that casual and traditional can mix together beautifully to create a unique space. The feature on *Traditional Home*'s "Built for Women" showhouse especially caught my eye. It was full of decorating ideas that I plan to use.

Danielle C
Aliso Viejo, Californ

Hearing from our readers is important to us. Send your comments to The Editor, Traditional Home *magazine, 1716 Locust St., Des Moines, IA 50309-3023, or fax us at* 800/513-2935. *You can also e-mail us at traditionalhome@mdp.com. We reserve the righ to edit letters for length, clarity, and style.*

The Crane Paper Company on writing and giraffes.

In a world where the mere appearance of a handwritten note in one's mailbox
is a bit of a surprise in itself, imagine finding a giraffe in there. But where is it written
that putting your thoughts down on paper has to be such a predictable or serious affair?
We hope a trip to one of our authorized Crane Retailers will provide more than simply
the touch and feel of uncommonly beautiful paper. We trust you'll find a surprise or two.

For the writer somewhere in each of us.™

Crane's ®

Fine French Linens for Bed, Bath & Table

ALABAMA

Birmingham · CHRISTINE'S (205) 871-8297
Mobile · THE GIVING TREE (888) 678-0068
Montgomery · HOME COUTURE (888) 545-4006
Tuscaloosa · THE LINEN CLOSET (800) 561-7331

ARIZONA

Scottsdale · NIGHT & DAY (480) 481-5106

CALIFORNIA

Beverly Hills · YVES DELORME (310) 550-7797
Burlingame · YVES DELORME (650) 342-6767
Calabasas · GRACIOUS ROOMS (818) 591-9777
La Jolla · EVERETT STUNZ CO., LTD. (800) 883-3305
Laguna Beach · LAGUNA COLONY CO. (949) 497-8919
Los Altos · COVER STORY (800) 944-4848
Los Gatos · THE MAIDS' QUARTERS, INC. (408) 395-1980
Malibu · MALIBU COLONY CO. (310) 317-0177
Modesto · LINO BELLA (209) 491-0931
Pasadena · SALUTATIONS HOME (626) 577-7460
Sacramento · CALLA LILY FINE LINENS (916) 564-1800
San Francisco · SCHEUER LINENS (800) 762-3950
Santa Rosa · REVERIE LINENS (800) 818-0008

COLORADO

Denver · THE BRASS BED (303) 322-1712
     AT HOME LINENS at Scandia Down (303) 355-8087

CONNECTICUT

Greenwich · LYNNENS, INC. (203) 629-3659
New Canaan · S. BROWNE & CO. (203) 966-2403
Westport · TOUCH OF EUROPE (203) 227-3355

DELAWARE

Wilmington · YVES DELORME (302) 656-3700

FLORIDA

Delray Beach · ABC CARPET & HOME (561) 279-7777
Jacksonville · THE BATH & LINEN SHOPPE (904) 398-7147
Miami · Dadeland Home Gallery BURDINES (305) 662-3532
Naples · GATTLE'S (800) 344-4552
Sarasota · YVES DELORME (941) 388-4494
South Miami · PACIFIC WHITE (305) 668-0882
St. Petersburg · GOOD NIGHT MOON (727) 898-2801
Tampa · VILLA ROSA DISTINCTIVE LINENS (813) 831-6189
Vero Beach · GATTLES (800) 243-4409
West Palm Beach · PIONEER LINENS (800) 207-5463
Winter Park · LUXE LINENS (407) 644-7677

GEORGIA

Atlanta · YVES DELORME PARK PLACE (678) 320-0097
     YVES DELORME VININGS (770) 438-7100
Roswell · THE CHANDLERY (800) 440-4789

ILLINOIS

Barrington · THE GILDED NEST (847) 381-6005
Chicago · ARRELLE FINE LINENS (800) 288-3696
     BEDSIDE MANOR, LTD. (773) 404-2020
Geneva · PAST BASKET (630) 232-4291
Hinsdale · BEDSIDE MANOR, LTD. (630) 655-0497
Lake Forest · MIMI'S LINGERIE & LINENS (847) 234-4050
Winnetka · BEDSIDE MANOR, LTD. (847) 441-0969

INDIANA

Indianapolis · THE WATER CLOSET (317) 849-1833

KANSAS

Overland Park · ANNABELLES (913) 345-0606

KENTUCKY

Louisville · BEDDED BLISS (502) 899-5153

LOUISIANA

Baton Rouge · CUSTOM LINENS (800) 808-0457
New Orleans · N.O. CUSTOM LINENS (504) 899-0604

MARYLAND

Annapolis · YVES DELORME (410) 224-0015
Baltimore · YVES DELORME (410) 828-4777
Bethesda · YVES DELORME (301) 897-5009

MASSACHUSETTS

Boston · LINENS ON THE HILL (617) 227-1255
Chestnut Hill · SCANDIA DOWN (617) 969-7990
Hingham · LA PETITE MAISON (781) 741-8393
Wellesley · BONSOIR (781) 416-2800
Yarmouthport · DESIGN WORKS (508) 362-9698

MICHIGAN

Birmingham · CRISTIONS (248) 723-3337
Grosse Pointe · KRAMER'S (800) 248-8906

MINNESOTA

Edina · EURO-AM BED & BATH CO. (952) 920-8038

MISSISSIPPI

Jackson · RAY'S FINE LINENS (800) 565-5206

MISSOURI

St. Louis · SALLIE (800) 257-9167

NEBRASKA

Omaha · THE LINEN GALLERY (402) 399-5242

NEW JERSEY

Far Hills · SYDNEY STREET (908) 781-0404
Long Beach Isl. · BETWEEN THE SHEETS (609) 361-9297
Madison · J&M HOME & GARDEN (800) 567-5268
Moorestown · LAVENDER'S (856) 608-1100
Pennington · ASHTON-WHYTE (609) 737-7171
Red Bank · DOWN TO BASICS (800) 822-2135
Saddle River · DETAILS & DESIGN (201) 825-4645
South Belmar · CLASSIC HOME (732) 280-7720
Upper Montclair · TESORI (973) 655-1511

NEW MEXICO

Santa Fe · DOWNTOWN BED & BATH (505) 988-4355

NEW YORK

New York · ABC CARPET & HOME (212) 473-3000
     GRACIOUS HOME (212) 988-8990
     HARRIS LEVY, INC. (212) 226-3102
     SCHWEITZER LINEN (212) 249-8361
Scarsdale · LA DENTELLIERE (914) 723-2902
Woodbury · ARTIFACTS, TOO (516) 364-6616

NORTH CAROLINA

Boone · DEWOOLFSON DOWN (800) 833-3696
Charlotte · BEDSIDE MANOR, INC. (704) 554-7727
Greensboro · COCOON (336) 275-4168
Pittsboro · THE COTTAGE SHOP (919) 545-9400
Raleigh · LAVENDER AND LACE (919) 828-6007
Wilmington · LINENS & LACE (910) 256-4824
Winston-Salem · BELLE MAISON (336) 722-8807

OHIO

Beachwood · YVES DELORME (216) 360-0285
Bexley · THE LINEN TREE (800) 480-3424
Cincinnati · GATTLE'S (800) 634-4369

OREGON

Portland · VIRGINIA JACOBS (503) 241-8436

OKLAHOMA

Oklahoma City · BELLE MAISON (405) 843-4611
Tulsa · THE DOLPHIN BED & BATH (918) 743-6634

PENNSYLVANIA

Buckingham · BIEN DORMIR (215) 794-9721
Haverford · YVES DELORME (610) 658-5510
Pittsburgh · FEATHERS (800) 382-9967
Reading · SYCAMORE SPRINGS (610) 926-3723
W. Bridgewater · BRIDGE STREET SHOP (724) 775-7131

RHODE ISLAND

Newport · RUE DE FRANCE (401) 846-3636

SOUTH CAROLINA

Charleston · YVES DELORME (843) 853-4331
Greenville · CHRISTA'S (864) 242-0025
Hilton Head · DEWOOLFSON DOWN (888) 833-3696

TENNESSEE

Chattanooga · YVES DELORME (423) 265-4005
Memphis · RÊVERIE Fine Linens & Down (800) 783-6188
Nashville · BELLA LINEA (615) 352-4041

TEXAS

Austin · PROVENÇAL HOME & GARDEN (512) 306-9449
Dallas · THE LINEN GALLERY (214) 522-6700
     YVES DELORME (214) 526-2955
Ft. Worth · YVES DELORME (817) 882-8531
Houston · LONGORIA COLLECTION (713) 621-4241
San Antonio · LIN MARCHÉ FINE LINENS (210) 826-677

UTAH

Salt Lake City · EUROPEAN LINENS (801) 575-8866

VERMONT

Manchester · YVES DELORME (802) 366-4974

VIRGINIA

Alexandria · YVES DELORME (703) 549-6660
Charlottesville · YVES DELORME (804) 979-4111
McLean · YVES DELORME (703) 356-3085
Richmond · YVES DELORME (804) 353-8701
Virginia Beach · YVES DELORME (757) 425-6963

WASHINGTON

Bellevue · SCANDIA DOWN (800) 309-3696
     YVES DELORME (425) 455-3508
Redmond · YVES DELORME (425) 881-1524
Seattle · YVES DELORME (206) 523-8407

WISCONSIN

Kohler · PAST BASKET (800) 401-9820

Yves Delorme®
PARIS
for
Palais Royal

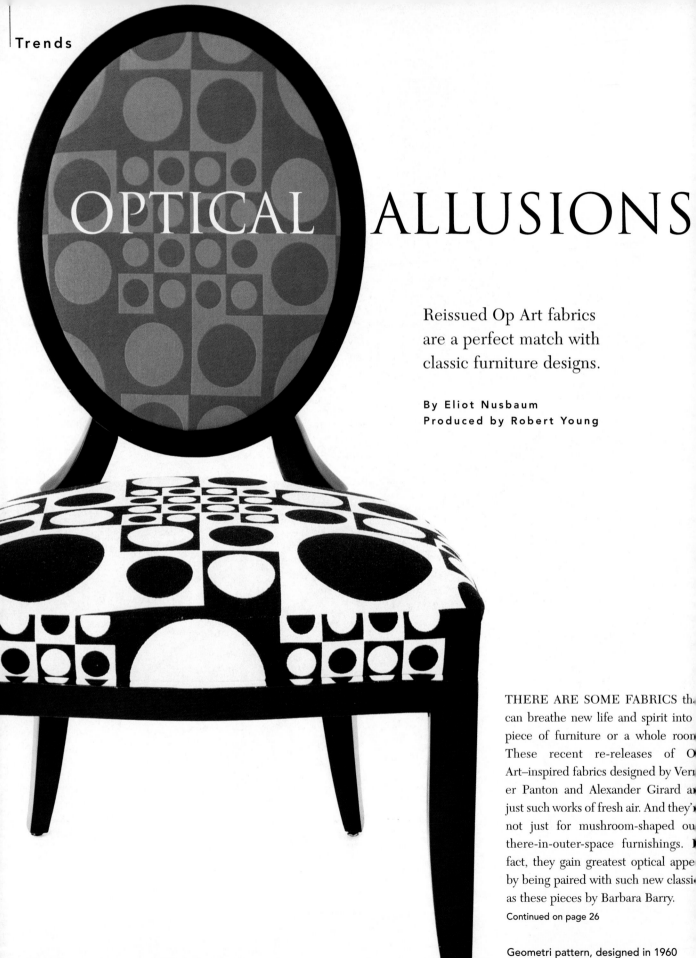

OPTICAL ALLUSIONS

Reissued Op Art fabrics
are a perfect match with
classic furniture designs.

By Eliot Nusbaum
Produced by Robert Young

THERE ARE SOME FABRICS th
can breathe new life and spirit into
piece of furniture or a whole roon
These recent re-releases of O
Art–inspired fabrics designed by Ver
er Panton and Alexander Girard a
just such works of fresh air. And they'
not just for mushroom-shaped ou
there-in-outer-space furnishings. I
fact, they gain greatest optical appe
by being paired with such new classi
as these pieces by Barbara Barry.

Continued on page 26

Geometri pattern, designed in 1960
by Verner Panton.

IT PRESENTS A STRONG ARGUMENT FOR BUYING POSTCARDS.

Introducing the 260-hp Acura TL Type-S. Attention shutterbugs: A bristling 3.2-liter V-6 and landscape photography just don't mix. So, as you engage its 5-speed Sequential SportShift™ automatic transmission, kindly suggest to your snap-happy passengers that they just relax and enjoy some tunes on the stereo. And leave the pictures to tripod-wielding professionals. ⒶACURA

Recently re-released Op Art fabric designed by Verner Panton and Alexander Girard are dynamic matches with any furniture style.

TRENDS Continued from page 24

These optical effects are brought to you by Maharam, the contract fabric company, as a part of its Textiles of the 20th Century series—the series that already has brought back the designs of Ray and Charles Eames and, recently, Anni Albers.

Panton (1926–1998), recognized not only for his fabrics but for his innovative furniture designs, worked for such well-known firms as Arne Jacobsen and Fritz Hansen in his native Denmark. His work was the subject of a recent internationally touring retrospective. Maharam has brought back two of his most popular fabric designs—Optik in six color combinations and Geometri in four colorways.

Girard (1907–1993) is known both as a designer and a collector of folk art. His vast folk-art collection is on display at the International Folk Art Museum in Santa Fe, where he lived. As a designer, he headed up the textile division of Herman Miller. Four of his best-known designs for the company have been brought back, including Checker Split, Double Triangles, and Facets, all of which are black and white, and Checker, which is available in six color combinations. Both the Panton and Girard fabrics are cotton/polyester blends and retail for about $100 a yard through designers. ⏍

Top left: Optik, designed in 1969, by Verner Panton. **Above:** Alexander Girard's Facets and Double Triangles, both designed in 1954.

For more information, see the Reader's Resource on page 188.

THE BUILT-IN ROLSCREEN® FROM PELLA.
DISAPPEARING SOON AT A WINDOW NEAR YOU.

Voila! It's down. And now, in the blink of an eye, it's up again. It can only be the Pella Rolscreen® window screen, the unique

retractable screen that's built right in. It works like a window shade for our casement windows, so there's no need to take it

out with the change of seasons. On a whim, you can simply unlatch it and have it out of sight, providing you with both an

unobstructed view and up to 40% more light. We thought it was a pretty bright idea. We think you'll agree. To find out more,

contact us at 1-800-54-PELLA or visit our website at www.pella.com.

VIEWED TO BE THE BEST.®

DOWN TO THE LAST INCH

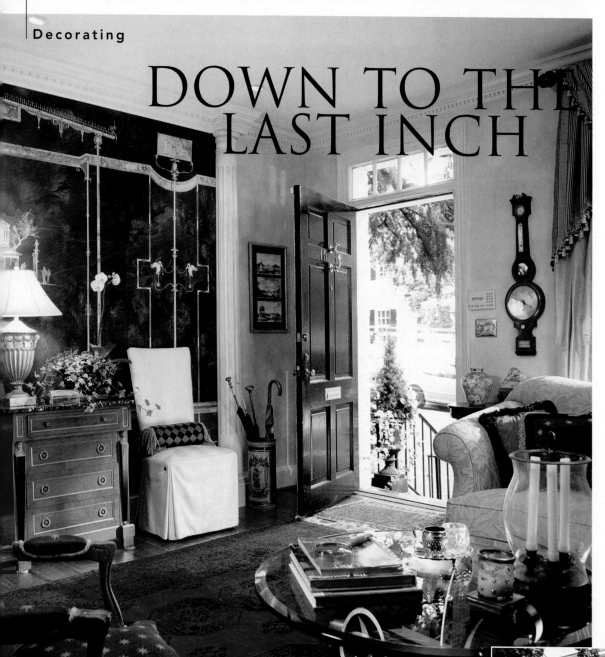

Left: Dixie Allen didn't approach her small house with a minimalist attitude. Instead, she filled the front room with stately objects while payi attention to color and texture to ma the overall design seem as open as possible.
Below: Every last inch of this Federa style row house wa meticulously plann for both style and function.

A tiny, Washington, D.C., row house lacks the expansive space of an average home but offers a plenitude of style and function.

By Krissa Rossbund

FOR MANY, the thought of a house only 20 feet wide brings on feelings of claustrophobia. The idea can conjure up too many bad memories of inefficient first homes, cramped dorm living, and even rooms shared with pesky siblings. But to Dixie Allen, diminutive spaces are delightful. Her positive outlook should come as no surprise to those familiar with her professional role as owner of Amazing Space Inc., a professional organizing service she founded in 1995.

While many would never have taken a second glance at a small vintage row house in Georgetown, Dixie looked at the space as the perfect opportunity to exercise her expertise. The result is a trim but tidy personal retreat that mixes elegance and efficiency.

Continued on page 30

PHOTOGRAPHER: ROSS CHA

DECORATING Continued from page 28

A longtime Washington, D.C., resident, she believes the main trick to functioning well is organization. Her clients—from homeowners overwhelmed by messy attics, closets, and cupboards to business owners buried under the trappings of booming success—can count on her to eliminate chaos with innovative solutions. "When we accumulate clutter, no matter how big the space is, we delay decision-making," she explains. "I get called when decisions can no longer be made."

With all this organization and efficiency, one might think Dixie's own home might be utilitarian and impersonal, but quite the opposite. She has filled the rooms with lav-

ish touches that transform each small into a work of beauty as well as an exa of efficient function. She even manage carve out an office in the tiny house so can work at home.

Such tight quarters are bound to c special problems, and this house wa exception. But with the help of long-friend and interior designer Beverly F Ritchie, she came up with a number of ative solutions.

For starters, because the living r also functions as a hallway and foye required a compact seating area that d interfere with the traffic flow to the c rooms. To that end, a camelback sofa teamed with a pair of armchairs as anc for the space. A pair of slipcovered arn chairs were placed nearby, making sea for seven an easy possibility.

Throughout the house, Dixie inco rated visual tricks to make the rooms r

Continued on page 32

Top: Dixie kept as much continuity between the rooms as possible. For example, she replicated the original living-room fireplace in the dining room and used variations of the same colors throughout the house. **Above:** In the back, a pergola was added to provide a shaded outdoor eating spot in the charming brick-paved garden area. Happy red-and-white-striped awnings shield the interior from the late-afternoon sun.

You Paid $300? Oops.

The prices some people charge for driving mocs, you'd think they'd throw in a set of tires. But that's the way it is with women's wear. High markups are the rule of the day.

At Lands' End, we take a more fair-minded approach. Our women's wear is just as reasonably priced as everything else we offer, because we skip the middlemen and designer logos.

Do we compromise on either quality or style? Never. Consider our Driving Mocs. Handstitched of fine leather, for a comfier fit. Fully leather lined. And fitted with long-wearing pebbled soles. All this in twelve colors to welcome spring, for just $79.

Same story with our Supima® Cotton Tees. Fine Gauge Cotton Twinsets. And hundreds more items that take you from weekends to workdays.

We always do our best to flatter you, too. Our women's pants are available in three distinct fits, to suit your shape or your mood. And we offer plenty of clothing in extended sizes with the same quality, style and value.

So call for a free catalog or click onto our Web site. No hassles, no headaches, and NO price games. It's the way shopping should be.

CALL OR CLICK 24 HOURS A DAY

1-800-960-9427   LANDSEND.COM

DECORATING Continued from page 30

expansive. In the living room's "entry area," a handsome, three-panel screen from Dixie's former residence was attached to the wall and framed by vertical columns on either side. Crown molding around the top of the wall makes the ceiling seem higher.

Another trick that helped stretch the living room was a rather elaborate window treatment. While one would think simplicity is best in a small house, Dixie and Ritchie proved otherwise. Lush, heavy fabrics hung directly below the crown molding were arranged to cover the wall and not the panes, making the window appear larger and more important.

In order to create some sense of continuity, one overall palette was developed, then applied to each room. "Dixie has a strong personality, so the colors needed to reflect that," says Ritchie. "People believe that you have to think small if you are living in a small space, but that's not true. You just need a flow of color that ties one room to the next so the eye is not distracted."

The main color used in the living room at the front of the house and kitchen/sitting room at the rear is a soft, creamy shade of off-white. Sandwiched between these two areas is the dining room, drenched in vibrant red. The backs of the living room's built-in bookshelves are painted the same red as the dining room's walls, and the creamy off-white of the living room walls is repeated in the woodwork and wainscoting of the dining room.

Originally, there were no windows to allow natural light into the dining room. Dixie knocked out one wall and inserted French doors that not only let in light but link the interior to the outdoor terrace garden. A simple, lacy, asymmetrical drapery panel dresses the doors without reducing

Continued on page 34

Top: The usual chandelier is missing from this dining room. Instead, sconces, art lights, natural lighting from a set of French doors, and sometimes a roaring fire provide plenty of light for this tiny room.
Inset: The vivacious Dixie Allen is savvy when it comes to organizing spaces without sacrificing style.

A flow of color to tie rooms together, mirrors, and crown moldings help make the house seem more expansive.

Above: A sponged finish in three shades of cream gives depth and texture to the living-room walls. The same treatment on the dining-room moldings and wainscoting ties the two spaces together.

DECORATING Continued from page 32

light. She also felt an overhead chandelier in the 13-square-foot dining room "cut into the space and made the already low ceiling appear even lower." So out went the chandelier and in came a large, oval mirror and a pair of sconces that bounce light back and forth, expanding the room with reflections.

Washington, D.C., is no joy for those who have a long commute to work, but for Dixie, traffic is rarely a concern. She transformed an existing nursery into an office, from which she runs her successful business. In such a condensed area, her only option was to add usable space vertically, so she wrapped the walls with custom storage,

files, and bookcases. A custom-fabrica[ted] desktop that can comfortably accommo[date] two people was also added. "I first asses[s] my needs, put together a wish list, and th[en] hoped that I could incorporate all th[e] things into the room's design," she says.

At the back of the house, the kitc[hen] and a former playroom were divided b[y a] wall with a small pass-through between. [By] removing the wall, Dixie was able to o[pen] up the kitchen and include a comforta[ble] sitting area.

With help from kitchen designer M[...] Kurtz, the organization expert got exac[tly] the type of kitchen she wanted—a su[...]

Continued on page 36

Left: Dixie Allen didn't give up be[au]ty for function. Cust[om] cherry cabinets a[nd] modern speckled granite offer the same kind of traditional style a[s] the formal dining room, seen throug[h] the kitchen door.

DECORATING Continued from page 34

efficient, U-shaped workspace, custom cherry cabinets that have the look of fine furniture, and a workable floor plan that allows traffic to flow from the front of the narrow house back to the kitchen and out to the garden without disturbing the cook. Luxurious granite was used for the countertops and backsplashes, and ample storage was incorporated on either side of the refrigerator and freezer.

In the adjoining sitting area, a window seat in the bay window was removed, making the perfect niche for a chair, ottoman, and side table. This allows a view of new, built-in bookcases, where lower cupboards disguise television and stereo equipment—yet another example of Dixie's inspired use of small spaces. 🛋

Interior designer: Beverly Flynn Ritchie
Regional editor: Eileen Deymier

For more information, see the
Reader's Resource on page 188.

Right: Like many people, Dixie uses her kitchen/sitting room more than any space in the house. The seamless transition between the two areas makes it easy to visit with guests and enjoy the garden view out the bay window while preparing a meal.

Alabama

Acton Flooring, Inc.
Birmingham
877-WOOL-RUG (877-966-5784)

Arizona

McFarland's Custom Carpets
Scottsdale
480-423-9155

Toliver's Carpet One
Tempe
480-777-5556

California

Abbey Carpet of San Francisco
San Francisco
415-752-6620

Beau Monde
South San Francisco
650-952-0119

Carousel Custom Floors
Pasadena
626-795-8085

Carpets & Floors, Inc.
Monterey
831-372-2300

Floor Styles
Cathedral City (Palm Springs)
760-324-1661

Lamorinda Floor Fashion
Lafayette
925-284-4440

Tuttle's Carpet One
Laguna Niguel
949-831-1332

Van Briggle Floors
Campbell
408-371-2003

Colorado

Balentine Collection
Aspen 970-925-4440
Breckenridge 970-453-5444

Connecticut

Kalamian's Rug Shop, Inc.
New London
860-442-0615

Morelli's Fine Floor Coverings
Ridgefield & New Canaan
203-431-9262

Florida

Crystal Tree Carpet
North Palm Beach
561-622-6333

Georgia

Bell Carpet Galleries
Atlanta
404-255-2431

Images Floor Coverings
Atlanta
404-876-6201

Myers Carpet
Atlanta 404-352-8141
Dalton 706-277-4053

Illinois

Carlson's Floors, Inc.
Geneva
630-232-4964

Central Rug &
Carpet Co., Inc.
Evanston
847-475-1190

D. Edmunds Interiors
& Floor Fashions
Burr Ridge
630-920-8900

DeSitter Carpet
and Rug, Inc.
LaGrange
708-352-3535
Carol Stream
630-653-5200

Lewis Carpet One
Northbrook
847-835-2400

Rexx Rug
Chicago
773-281-8800

Village Carpets
Chicago 773-935-8500
Winnetka 847-446-3800

Indiana

Lagemann Carpet, Inc. dba
The Carpet Craftsman
Fort Wayne
219-490-3655

Kansas

Carpet Corner
Kansas City Area
800-365-2102

Louisiana

LaCour's Carpet World
Baton Rouge
225-927-4130

Maine

Downeast Rug Co.
Portland
207-775-7818

Massachusetts

Faber's Rug Co., Inc.
Wellesley
800-698-3223

Harry's Carpet One
Quincy
617-328-4002

Landry & Arcari
Salem
800-649-5909

Michigan

McLaughlin's Home
Furnishing Designs
Southgate
734-285-5454

Riemer Floors, Inc.
Bloomfield Hills
248-335-3500

Missouri

Design Gallery*
Kansas City
816-753-3160

New Hampshire

Concord Carpet Center
Oriental Rugs & Carpeting
Concord
603-225-6600

New Jersey

Kaprelian Oriental Rugs
and Carpets
Ridgewood
877-644-5306

Rug & Kilim Carpet
Short Hills 973-467-1820
Morristown 973-425-2800

New York

A-1 Interior Carpets
New York City
212-734-8929

Carpet Trends
Rye
800-878-5188

Country Carpet & Rug
Syosset
516-822-5855

Data Carpet and Rug
New Hyde Park
516-352-8700

Designers North Carpet, Inc.*
Albertson
516-484-6161

Einstein Moomjy
New York City & New Jersey
800-864-3633

Sam's Floor Covering
White Plains
914-948-7267

Ohio

WCCV Flooring Design Center
Stow
330-688-0114
North Canton
330-494-4726

Oregon

Atiyeh Brothers Rugs & Carpets
Portland
503-639-8642

Pennsylvania

Barb-Lin Carpet One
Doylestown
215-348-8116

Tennessee

Myers Carpet
Nashville
615-777-3344

Texas

CDC Carpets & Interiors
Austin
512-327-8326

Emmet Perry & Co.*
Houston 713-961-4665
Austin 512-323-5503

Interior Resources*
Dallas
214-744-5740

Refined Flooring Limited
San Antonio
210-930-4966

Schroeder Carpet & Drapery
Austin
512-462-1551

Truett Fine Carpets and Rugs*
Dallas
214-748-7550

Venetian Blind & Floor
Carpet One
Houston
713-528-2404

Virginia

Carpet One of Alexandria
Alexandria
703-370-0000

Washington

M.G. Whitney & Co.
Issaquah
425-369-8100

Washington, D.C.

Classic Floor Designs, Inc.
Washington, D.C.
202-872-9860

WOOLS OF NEW ZEALAND®

THE STANDARD OF EXCELLENCE IN WOOL CARPETS

YOUR FAVORITE

WOOL BLANKET.

SQUARED.

On your body or on your floor, nothing looks, feels or endures like wool. For fashionable and long-lasting wool carpet, look for the Wools of New Zealand Brand. The Standard of Excellence in Wool Carpets and Rugs. See the retailers and trade showrooms listed on the opposite page or visit us at www.woolsnz.com.

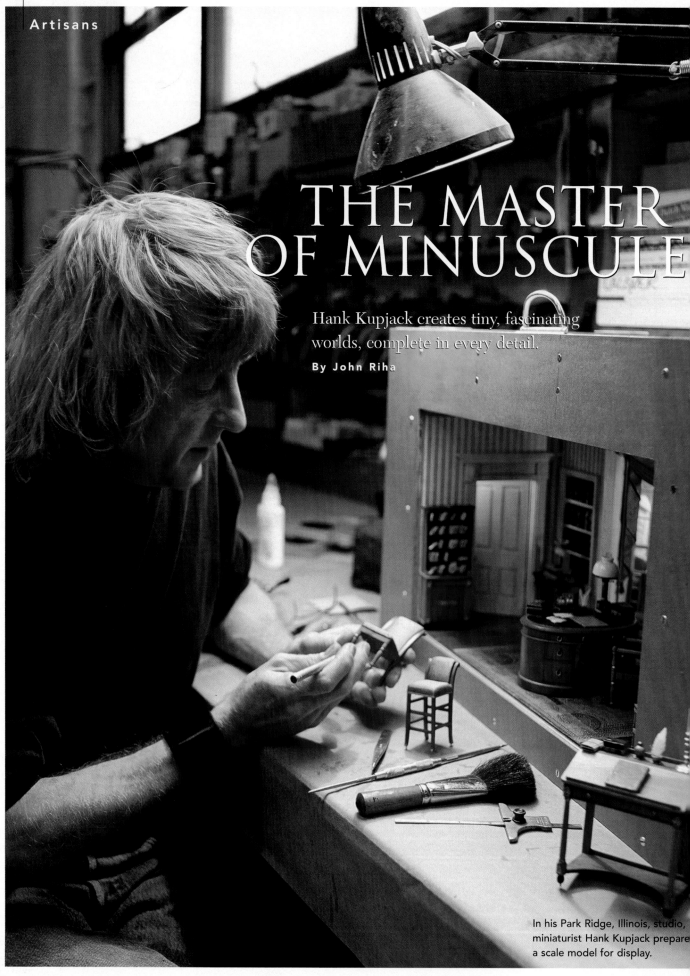

THE MASTER
OF MINUSCULE

Hank Kupjack creates tiny, fascinating
worlds, complete in every detail.

By John Riha

In his Park Ridge, Illinois, studio,
miniaturist Hank Kupjack prepare
a scale model for display.

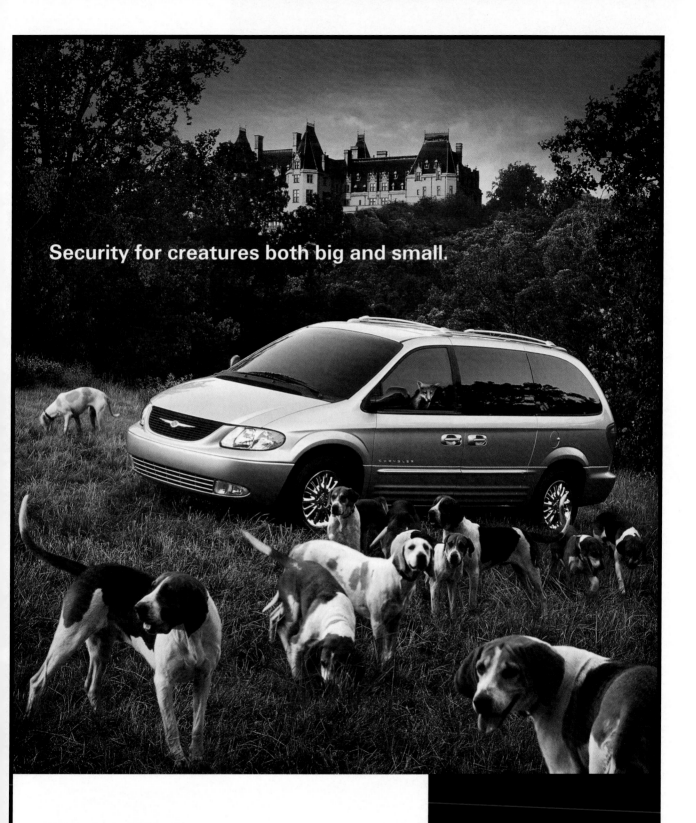

Security for creatures both big and small.

TOWN & COUNTRY

Now enter a safe haven from life's challenges. Town & Country, re-engineered, redesigned with minivan firsts. 1.800.CHRYSLER or www.chrysler.com. **Town & Country, the best minivan ever.***

CHRYSLER

Left: The final touch—Kupjack uses tweezers to add an individually folded letter to a 1:12 scale Regency filing cabinet. The cabinet belongs in a room model depicting an English barrister's office. **Below:** Kupjack seated in front of several of his many miniature rooms. **Bottom:** One of Kupjack's most popular creations is a reproduction of a 1950s diner, complete with lots of chrome, napkin holders, sugar shakers, ashtrays, and salt and peppers.

WELCOME TO THE WORLD of Hank Kupjack. It's a small-minded place, but that's no reflection on him. Light coming through dusty windows set high in the wall catches lazy vines of smoke twisting up from a cigarette balanced at the edge of a well-worn workbench. Tweezers in one hand, rare 19th-century English Regency filing cabinet nestled in the palm of the other, he gives a bemused smile and shakes his shaggy head.

"It's hard to explain to people what I do," he says. "Most of my friends don't give a damn about it."

One thing is certain: Kupjack is a rare breed. Few artisans anywhere do what he does, and only a handful do it with as much skill and élan. Kupjack is a miniaturist, but the description falls well short of indicating the spectrum of his abilities. There are many professional miniaturists, but most specialize in a particular genre, such as making furniture or casting metal. Kupjack does it all. Diminutive mahogany chests and chairs, elaborately curved balustrades, gilded mirrors, porcelain bathroom fixtures, silver tea sets, faux-marbled columns and floors, china creamers, and leather-bound books are all produced by Kupjack's hand in 1:12 scale. Each piece is then carefully positioned in dioramic boxes to form re-creations of exotic venues—anything from Alexander the Great's siege tent to the Colonial-style dining room from Kupjack's boyhood home. In the process, the artisan must blend an encyclopedic knowledge of architectural history with a surgeon's dexterity and a set designer's cunning.

Continued on page 44

*Stylish yet timeless, elegant yet practical
and built to be used...everyday.*

*Vibrant prints, colorful plaids and correlating solids
illustrate the attention to detail and design
that is expressed by quality craftsmanship.*

King Hickory...a tradition of style, quality and comfort.

KING HICKORY FURNITURE

For more information, or a dealer near you, call 1.800.337.8827 www.kinghickory.com

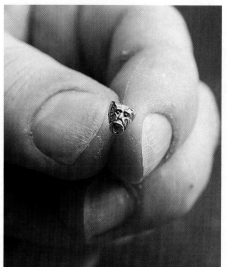

ARTISANS Continued from page 42

He learned the miniaturist's art from his father. The late Eugene Kupjack was recognized as the world's preeminent maker of miniature rooms. Kupjack père created a sensation in the 1930s and '40s as principal builder of a series of room sets for Mrs. James Ward Thorne, daughter-in-law of the founder of Montgomery Ward. Those 68 rooms, depicting eras of gracious European and American living, are known collectively as the Thorne Miniature Rooms and are on display at the Art Institute of Chicago.

On any given day of the week, you're likely to find Hank Kupjack bending to some tiny task in the Park Ridge, Illinois, shop where he's worked for more than 20 years. The expansive workplace, once a DeSoto car dealership, is brimming with the implements and accoutrements of the miniaturist's art. A room devoted to woodworking bristles with bench tools and stacks of the cherry and maple needed to produce

fine, fool-the-eye grain patterns. Anc area is devoted to metal-casting, w petite moldings, ornaments, and table are carved and cast from tin, lead, b gold, and silver. Everywhere are dra and bins filled with additional parts pieces—fabrics with appropriately sc patterns for use as drapery and uphols boxes of glass beads for making cha liers; collections of tiny statues plu from flea markets and secondhand st scenic newsprint advertisements, sele for their matte finish, that are destine become wall murals in the courts of ki

Rulers, calipers, and dividers are tered about, but Kupjack rarely relie mechanical means to divine correct s "I can pretty much tell what's proportic ly correct just by looking at it," he "You can drive yourself crazy fussing ov fraction of an inch that becomes u tectable to the human eye."

"I get a little tired of hearing, 'Oh, must be so hard!' and 'How can you s working on things that are so small?' " fesses Kupjack with a shrug. "To tell the truth, I've been at it so long, it do seem that difficult. At the same time,

Continued on page 46

Below: Eugene Kupjack made a reproduc of the family dining room, right down to family portraits hanging on the wall.
Top left: A lion's-head drawer pull in Fren Empire style was cast in solid, 18-karat go
Far left: Petit-point rugs copy floor coveri used in Pullman railroad cars in the late 18 and feature 1,600 stitches per square inch
Left: Chairs carved in the Victorian Empire style are for the Pullman railway car.

create.

ARTISANS Continued from page 44

job is a new challenge; nothing is the same from job to job. That's why I enjoy doing it."

The Thorne Rooms created by his father represent his introduction to the world of miniatures. As a child, he and his younger brother, Jay, often accompanied his father on trips to the Thorne studio to review progress on the rooms. He well remembers the elderly Mrs. Thorne.

"She sent down to Brooks Brothers and had outfits made up for us," recalls Kupjack. "Gray flannel suits, Sherlock Holmes outfits, and red-and-white seersucker suits with straw hats. We had to wear them whenever we went to visit her."

Undeterred by such strictures, Kupjack would find his way to his father's shop to make wagons and other toys. At 14, he was allowed to do wall painting and other basic set decorations. As a young man, he tried stints as an architect and rock musician but kept returning to the craft his father taught him. Over the years, he assisted his dad in the construction of more than 600 miniature rooms, some destined for the homes of such notables as Marshall Field IV, actress Helen Hayes, and department store mogul Donald Dayton.

Today, the conservation of older Kupjack creations that reside at the Baltimore Museum of Art, Winterthur, the Illinois State Museum, and private collections, makes up a large portion of Hank Kupjack's business. Although the rooms are occasionally damaged due to mishandling, the most insidious culprit is dust, drawn into the boxes from heat convection generated by

the little stage lights that illuminate each set. Kupjack now defeats dust by sealing lights inside Plexiglas tubes.

Kupjack has also produced more than 50 rooms of his own. His current works include an 1892 Pullman Company railroad observation car, an 1885 San Franciscan saloon, and the conservation and completion of five Kupjack rooms soon to be on permanent display at The New Naples Museum of Art in Naples, Florida.

"We're thrilled to have them," says Myra Janco Daniels, CEO of the Naples museum. "Hank is a fantastic artist; it's amazing how much people enjoy his work. Before I became familiar with these rooms, I never truly appreciated miniatures. I do now."

Continued on page 48

Above: An English Regency music room features an orn upright piano. This room is on temporary display at The New Naples Museum c Art in Naples, Florida. **Left and below:** Items of precio gold and silver, such as delicate candlesticks and te services, are cast by the los wax process. In the 1940s and '50s, the Kupjacks mad patterns for metal miniature More than 250,000 were made and sold individually before metal prices escalate beyond profitability.

bruce.com
1-800-722-4647
For the Master Showcase
Dealer nearest you.

ashionable. Affordable. Practical.

Bruce.
hardwood floors
from (A)rmstrong

Top: This copy of a modern, antiques-filled Parisian apartment features a mix of Louis XV and Louis XVI styles. **Above:** Vignettes of fabulous interior design—from the raw splendor of Alexander the Great's war tent to the courtly magnificence of an 18th-century Louis XVI dining room—are on display in the vault room at the Kupjack studio.

ARTISANS Continued from page 46

Historically, the art world has never fully embraced miniatu known in gallery parlance as "three-dimensional constructio mixed media." Kupjack shrugs off the snub. "There's no art so associated with miniatures," he notes. "Without a scene, few leries are willing to take them on." He adds that the price of a gle example ranges from $30,000 to $65,000, placing miniat toward the high end of specialty art items. "My dad sold his a antiques store in Chicago," Kupjack explains. "Back then, pric $1,500 were more what you might expect."

As to the mesmerizing effect of miniatures, Kupjack m "There's an innocence about them. It's like playing with a toy w you were a child, and you fill in whatever's missing to make a world of your own. In these rooms, the blanks are filled in, but effect is the same. You can't help but be delighted and surpris

And how. Stare long enough at the 1810 English Regency s shop and its display cases filled with dozens of handcra tureens, candlesticks, sconces, and tea services, and you're rea reach for your drawstring purse. Or stop by the 1950s diner cheeseburger and a shake. While you wait, drop a nickel in jukebox and twirl around on the counter stools. At this diner coffee is always hot, and the hand-stitched, black leather ja draped over the chrome coatrack is very cool indeed.

"The '50s diners are some of the most popular rooms I ma says Kupjack, who stylizes the boxes surrounding these Elvis miniatures by finishing the cases with rounded Deco corners flashy chrome accents. Asked if he has a personal favorite fror the sets he's made, Kupjack has a sly smile and a ready ans "Usually," he grins, "it's the one I've just sold." 🏛

For more information, see the Reader's Resource on page 188.

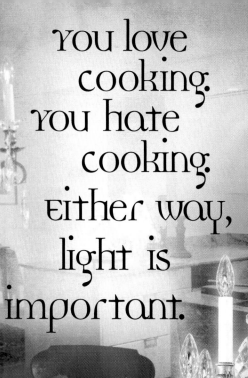

you love
cooking.
you hate
cooking.
Either way,
light is
important.

So many
memories color the
kitchen. Visions of yourself
as a small child waiting for cookies.
Images of dinners inspired by love, and
dinners that were dreary obligations. Flashbacks of
impassioned politics at the kitchen table.

Let others treat the kitchen as a food factory. You who understand its
emotional resonance will want something meaningful to look at, as you pause
between mixing and marinating.

Renaissance by Schonbek is a seventeenth-century style favored by Louis XIV, a French
monarch who loved to plot and play by the light of magnificent crystal chandeliers.
Despite its royal antecedents, Renaissance has an air of fun
that suits an eclectic kitchen.

Schonbek has been making crystal chandeliers since 1870 in Bohemia.
Call us for a free Schonbek video.

CRAIG PONZIO
CUSTOM FRAME COLLECTION

LARSON·JUHL

CUSTOM FRAME THE BEAUTY OF YOUR HOME

PUTTING THE "ENGLISH" ON IVY

For the sin of being serviceable, ivy is often taken for granted. Yet, with a connoisseur's approach, it rises to a host of occasions.

By Mitchell Owens and Elvin McDonald

PERT, DEPENDABLE, OH SO TIDY ivy has become the horticultural poster child for genteel mediocrity. Even the normally spirited *Oxford English Dictionary* has trouble mustering up much enthusiasm in its definition of the world's favorite vine: "a well-known climbing evergreen shrub...indigenous to Europe and parts of Asia and Africa."

Once upon a time, however, the genus *Hedera* had a spicy reputation. Sacred to Bacchus, the god of the cocktail hour, ivy was considered a cure-all for any hangover. Toga-clad party animals suffering from morning-after headaches often lay abed, tiaras of ivy gently draped over their throbbing temples. That lusty imagery survived well into the Middle Ages, when taverns and public houses with choice stocks of wine advertised their liquid wares by nailing a garland of ivy to the front door.

Somewhere along the line, however, ivy entered a 12-step program and turned over a new leaf. Church artisans co-opted the evergreen pagan plant, transforming it into a symbol of heavenly love everlasting. Poets composed paeans to its cling-

Continued on page 54

Circles of all sizes are easiest way to train ivy The collection here, at the home of Evelyn ar Jim Maddux in Camar California, adds panac to an old kitchen cabi

THIBAUT

Wallpaper & Fabrics Since 1886

Thibaut wallpaper and fabrics are available through designers, showrooms and fine retail stores.
Ask for Thibaut (pronounced Tee bo). For availability in your area, call **800-223-0704.**

English ivy has a fluid quality that lets it take on endless decorative forms and shapes.

GARDENS Continued from page 52

Top left: Ivy topiaries add a stylish touch to garden table. **Above:** Floral designer Betsy Williams of Andover, Massachusetts, favors cream- and gold-variegated ivy for a bridal bouquet featuring roses and rosemary. **Left** Ivy growing in the ground on the other side of the wall is threaded through holes to for garlands in a Los Angeles garden. **Below le** New Bedford, Massachusetts, plantsman Allen Haskell chose a tiny-leafed bird's-foot ivy to clothe a peacock-shaped wire form.

ing nature. By the time Charles Dickens dubbed it "a dainty plant" in his 1837 novel *Pickwick Papers*, ivy's rehabilitation was complete. Today, when not sweetly trained into cones or spheres, ivy is used as camouflage, cloaking walls or substituting for grass in areas of deep shade.

But ivy has more going for it than its cultural propriety and reputation for unrelieved green would suggest. Algerian ivy combines emerald leaves with wine-dark twigs. *H. canariensis* 'Gloire de Marengo' is boldly variegated, mottled like cream splashed onto green leather. Grown in full sun, *H. helix* 'Buttercup' is dairy yellow.

According to the latest botanical count, 11 species of the genus *Hedera* have been identified, and six are in cultivation. *H. helix*, common or English ivy, is far and away the most popular, and it shares with all the others the same trait of having two life stages, juvenile and adult. In the juvenile stage, the lobe-leafed vines trail, creeping across the ground or climbing by means of aerial roots. In a garden setting, when an

ivy reaches the top of a wall or high int tree, topping out into full sun, it tends manifest the adult stage, in the proc becoming shrublike and producing p leaves instead of the lobed juvenile ones

In the adult stage, ivies also bloom a bear fruit, but their seeds are not source of new ivies. Considering that recently as 1974, when the American Society was formed, there were only ab 60 different ivies being grown commerc ly and now there are nearly 500, fr whence came these new cultivars?

Spontaneous mutation is the answ The ivy is a sporting plant, especially wh it is growing luxuriantly. When large nu bers of ivies are being cultivated, the obs vant grower is inevitably going to spy fr time to time a new shoot that is differen size, shape, or coloration from all the oth on the same plant. If a cutting takes and forms a plant displaying in a sta fashion what is new, the grower will giv a name and multiply stocks for introduct into the nursery trade.

Continued on page 56

t's a great night for a campfire.

Left: A quartet of 8-inch wreaths, done in different ivies and planted in similar 6-inch pots, brings life to a gilt étagère. Trained ivies will grow well almost indefinitely indoors in bright indirect sunlight or good reading light. Keep the soil evenly moist and give the leaves a refreshing shower at the sink every week or so.

THE 3-MINUTE IVY WREATH

Ready-made ivy wreaths are commonly availab in flower shops and garden centers—for a pric You can fashion your own in minutes by startir with a purchased ivy hanging basket. Select a plant that has long strands, preferably 15 inch long or longer. Add a wire circle, which can be shaped from a clothes hanger. Use a decorativ pot as a slipcover for the grower's pot, and vc you are ready to wind the ivy up, up, and awa

GARDENS Continued from page 54

While an ivy is an ivy is an ivy to the untrained eye, connoisseurs can spot minute differences in leaf shape, size, and coloration, as well as habit, from 60 paces and name names. To help the novice sort out the plethora of new ivies in the marketplace, and to feel excitement about the possibilities rather than confused, the American Ivy Society recognizes seven distinct categories.

1. Curlies—for example, 'Parsley Crested.' Aptly named, this cultivar has rounded leaves that are wavy and crimped at the edges. It is self-branching and throws long trails that make it ideal for spilling over the edges of any container or for training as a 12-inch or larger wreath. 'Maureena,' which has large green, gray, and white leaves, is a superb example of a variegated curly ivy.

2. Bird's foot—for example, 'Anita,' which is also considered a miniature. Some leaves on each strand have five sharply pointed lobes that suggest the imprint of a bird's foot; others have a central lobe with distinctive "teeth" about two-thirds of the way from the tip. The plant grows slowly but is also strongly self-branching. It is suited to training as a small topiary or hanging basket.

3. Heart shapes—for example, 'Christian.' This small cultivar is given to producing both heart-shaped and slightly three-lobed leaves. Untrained, it is perfect as a spot of green in a cachepot placed within the circle of brightest light under a table lamp. 'Christian' is also ideal for training on any small topiary form.

4. Fans—for example, 'Boskoop,' which has broadly diamond-shaped leaves that may be one- to three-lobed with tightly frilled margins. The zigzagging of the stems and relatively distant spacing of the leaves along them make it adaptable to a variety of uses.

5. Oddities—for example, 'Fallen Angel.' This is something of a catchall category for ivies that don't fit neatly elsewhere. 'Fallen

Continued on page 58

1. Remove hangers from the growing pot and slip the pot inside a slightly larger decorative pot, one with a drainage hole if the ivy is to be displayed outdoors.

2. Take a wire clothes hanger and bend it into a circle. Insert the hook end into the center of the ivy pot. Select strands of ivy and wind them, one at a time, around the circle.

3. Continue winding strands of ivy up and around the circle until the desired fullness is achieved. Let unused strands of ivy cascade all around the pot rim.

Introducing the revolutionary *GE Profile Arctica*™ Refrigerator.

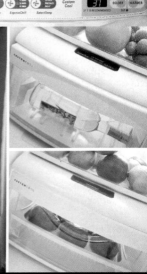

The GE Profile Arctica™ Refrigerator with CustomCool™
technology does things that no ordinary refrigerator can.
It lets you customize the temperature of
whatever you put in it. So you can
chill wine in minutes.
Or thaw meat in half the time.
The Arctica refrigerator can even fill tall glasses with
extra ice, extra fast.
And makes living in a very fast world a lot easier.

Profile™

We bring good things to life.

Above: The eight different ivies and topiary forms offered on this page as separate collections (right) are shown after about six months of growing and training.

GARDENS Continued from page 56

Angel' has closely set, spirally arranged three-lobed leaves on flattened stems. Except for its vigorous growth habit, this small-leafed ivy would likely be classified as a miniature. It's wonderful for hanging baskets or for any small topiary form.

6. Ivy ivies—those with typical ivy leaves that are palmately five-lobed, the middle one being more prominent.

7. Miniatures—for example, 'Cascade.' These have leaves less than 1 inch long and of any shape. Excepting size, 'Cascade' could easily be taken as an "ivy ivy." Long, trailing stems make it ideal for hanging baskets or for any wreath or topiary training.

'Lady Frances,' the 2001 Ivy of the Year, is a superb example of a variegated miniature. The variably shaped small leaves are a combination of gray, white, and green and the plants grow exuberantly. 'Lady Frances' is suited to any ivy use, indoors or out.

An efficient, fun way you can become acquainted with the different types of ivy is to grow a collection that includes one of each. If you start training them when they are small, potted topiaries are endlessly satisfying as decorative objects. To hold strands in place, they can be wrapped around the form and tucked under each other. Errant strands can be made to conform by encircling them with short lengths of green-painted florist wire. Joining the ivy league will give you hours of pleasure from minutes of gardening and produce living emblems of virtue, prosperity, and beneficence. 🏛

For information about the American Ivy Society, write to P.O. Box 2123, Naples, FL 34106-2123, or go to www.ivy.org.

English Ivy to Go

Available exclusively to the readers of *Traditional Home®* magazine, each ivy collection contains eight plants, one each of those shown below. They are, left to right: back row—'Boskoop,' 'Maureena,' 'Cascade,' and 'Parsley Crested'; front row—'Christian,' 'Anita,' 'Fallen Angel,' and 'Lady Frances' (2001 Ivy of the Year).

Each ivy plant will be shipped in a 4-inch pot and will be about 5 to 7 inches tall at the time of shipment.

By special arrangement with Seaview Nursery, shipments of ivy collections will be made until mid November 2001, while supplies last. Please order early; we ship on a first-come, first-served basis. Each collection costs $54.95, which includes shipping by Federal Express 2-Day service, handling, and applicable sales tax. Sorry, we are unable to ship to Alaska, Hawaii, Puerto Rico, Mexico, or Canada.

Our topiary wire-frame collection, from Pacific Wire & Supply Inc., includes one each of the following designs: Spiral (15 inches tall), Parsol (16 inches tall), Flame (12 inches tall), Large Ivy Hoop (12 inches in diameter), Small Ivy Hoop (6 inches in diameter), Topiary Ball (13 inches tall with a 4-inch ball), Tree (10 inches tall), and Obelisk (12 inches tall). All have been scaled to use with 5- to 7-inch pots. The complete collection of eight frames cost $79.95, which includes shipping by UPS ground service, handling, and applicable sales tax. Sorry, we are unable to ship to Alaska, Hawaii, Puerto Rico, Mexico, or Canada.

TO ORDER with your MasterCard, Visa, or Discover card, call toll free 800/848-0115. To order by mail, specify the number of ivy collections desired and topiary frame collections you wish to purchase. Then calculate the total and send a check or money order to: Traditional Home Shopping Service, Dept. 010, Box 9297, Des Moines, IA 50306-9297.

HEAVEN DOES EXIST
AND IS AVAILABLE IN TEN FINISHES

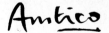

IT'S A SMALL WORLD

Playhouses in Connecticut, Pennsylvania, and
Iowa fire the imaginations of children
and maybe even their parents.

By Eliot Nusbaum

Taylor and Spencer Rinfret
and their golden retriever,
Sconset, enjoy a little away
time in their playhouse.
The house came as a
prefab stock playhouse
but was customized to
look more like their home.

PHOTOGRAPHER: BOB MA

25 years of stain protection.

You'll need it.

We have just the carpet to help you through her next 25 years. Click on leesforliving.com to learn all about it.

Carpet has come a long way in the last few years. And LEES For Living® is leading the way, with its superior design, advanced technology, and the first and only 25-year stain warranty.* That's why, if you're shopping for carpet for your home right now, you really must do yourself this favor. Go to leesforliving.com and see our remarkable demonstration. You'll find out what makes this unique carpet perfect for a growing family. You'll also find an incredible SPECIAL OFFER.

*See store for details.

EVEN THOUGH SPENCER and Ta
Rinfret are getting a little old for their p
house, they still spend a lot of time th
Their mother, Cindy, thinks it's because
playhouse is a part of the whole envi
ment of their Connecticut property and
just pushed aside into an isolated corne
the yard. To help the playhouse fit into
environment, it was painted the same w
with green shutters as the Rinfrets' "
house. Plus it was landscaped to fit into
Rinfrets' gardens, with flowering plan
the planters and window boxes, stone s
statuary, and delightful miniature out
furniture. By planning the playhouse a
integral part of the gardens, Cindy beli
it added to the overall feel of the exte
space, a bit like a folly. It helps, too, tha
interior of the 8x10-foot structure i
warm and friendly as the children's
rooms; in fact, the playhouse is furnishe
part with items from their rooms. Addir
the charm inside is a hand-painted sisal
a collection of antique wicker, and cust
made and upholstered pieces designe
Cindy, who has her own interior de
company—a true house in miniat

One look at the place, outside or i
enough to melt your heart. It is the pe
getaway for a child.

Regional editor: Bonnie Maharam
Continued on page 66

Spencer and Taylor
Rinfret's playhouse began
life as a standard pre-cut
kit, delivered by truck.
But touches from home—
including the table and
chairs, play dishes, and
stuffed animals—mixed
with antiques, custom-
upholstered pieces, a
painted sisal rug and
delightful framed prints
make it something
very special.

You work hard

for your piece of the pie.

You shouldn't have to worry about crumbs.

Make cleaning a little easier
with the exclusive 8 rotating brush system from Hoover.
(6 brushes in the nozzle, 2 more on the powered hand tool.)

The Hoover® SteamVac™ Widepath™ cleans a big, 14-inch path so you can scrub away dirt and spills from your carpet quickly.

And with its Clean Surge™ feature, you can spray additional cleaning solution on hard-to-clean areas.

So now, you can take some of the "work" out of your housework.

HOOVER

DEEP DOWN, YOU WANT HOOVER.™

The SteamVac™ Widepath™ from Hoover.

www.hoover.com

With their sons in mind, Michael and Nadine Kastner thought it would be fun to design and build a unique playhouse.

PERSONAL ARCHITECTURE
Continued from page 64

ASK AN ARCHITECT and his design wife to design a playhouse for their kid and you can pretty well figure you're goin to get something special. And sure enoug when Michael and Nadine Kastner set o to build such a structure for their two son Joe and Ian, they came up with somethin that was both fun and unique. Not too su prisingly, it also is a good architectural with their 1920s-era Craftsman-style hom located in an older neighborhood in D Moines, Iowa.

In keeping with the general feel of the bungalow, the Kastners designed the pla house with materials that are consiste with their home and the way it is co structed. Explains Michael, "I wanted th playhouse design to express how things together. I designed it so the structur materials are totally exposed and also ble with different textures." So, the tile-li black-and-red corrugated asphalt roof ha low pitch like the house and, like the hous exposed structural elements. Cedar plan and copper tubing on the ladder, too, a derived from the Craftsman vernacular.

But, of course, the Kastner boys are least as engaged by the slide and sandb and rightly so.

Regional editor: Deb Riha

Continued on page 68

The fort-like playhouse, designed by Michael and Nadine Kastner for their sons Joe, **above**, and Ian, is an open structure raised above a sandbox. Detailing such as the cross-patterned floor, exposed-beam ceiling and copper tube ladder rungs all reflect the Craftsman style of the family home.

PHOTOGRAPHER: DOUG SN

life stuff storage

Where do you put the stuff that you're about? All that you are? Tell us. We're listening.
And this is how we start to create your custom solution.

Call us for your complimentary in-home consultation at 800.336.9188
in the US and Canada or visit us at www.calclosets.com.

CALIFORNIA CLOSETS®

PERSONAL ARCHITECTURE
Continued from page 66

STEPHEN PENNELL was driv[ing] home to the Philadelphia area fr[om] California when he made a stop [in] Pittsburgh. While there, he visited [the] Frick House Museum and saw a g[reat] little children's playhouse on [the] grounds of the museum. Thinking [it] would be fun to build one himself, [he] decided to do a playhouse for his [sis]ter's kids. He enjoyed the whole p[ro]cess so much, he gave up teach[ing] math and started building playhou[ses] full-time. In the six years since, he [has] sold more than 60 Gothic cottages [and] Gothic villas, Italianate villas, [and] Greek Revival pl[ay]houses through[out] the country. The [de]signs are inspired [by] the real thing. [For] example, the Go[thic] villa pictured [on] this page is base[d on a] 19th-century ho[me] in Cape May, N[ew] Jersey, and the [Ital]ianate Villa is m[od]eled on a home n[ear] where he grew [up.] "I walked past [it] every day and [was] always inspired [by] that home," rec[alls] Stephen, who [has] made a hobby [of] 18th- and 19th-c[en]tury architect[ure.] He does all [the] work on his p[lay]houses himself [and] then delivers [and] assembles them [on] site. The minia[ture] houses cost f[rom] $3,500 to $8,5[00.] One customer [was] so enthusiastic, [he] bought five of [the] playhouses and g[ave] them to friends [on] Martha's Vineya[rd.]

Stephen is [cur]rently working [on a] Georgian-style [play]house to add to his line, and a Qu[een] Anne-style playhouse is in the plan[ning] stage. His line can be seen on his W[eb] site at www.little-mansions.com.

Left: Stephen Pennell's nieces, Abigail and Catherine Miller, enjoy tea and a good read inside the Gothic Villa playhouse, **below and bottom left,** their uncle built for them. The success of this first version inspired Stephen to start a whole line of playhouses.

The playhouses are finished with colorful floors and painted beams inside and gingerbread trim, finials, and ironwork on the exterior. The attention to detail captures the essence of a period, while the scale places each playhouse squarely in the realm of make-believe.
Left: Emma and Catherine Miller

For more information, see the Reader's Resource on page 188.

The **Style** you want, the **Comfort** you expect, and the **Quality** you deserve.

homecrest®
Casual and Outdoor Furniture

To experience Homecrest fine furniture, visit your local authorized dealer. To find the dealer nearest you, or for a Free brochure, call us at 888-346-4852, or visit our web site at www.homecrest.com.

Address: Box 350, Wadena, MN 56482 **Phone:** 1-888-346-4852 **Web Site:** www.homecrest.com

STUNNING...

Heritage from The Golden Age Rug Collection by

SAMAD

PALACE PORCELAIN

The red, blue, and gold porcelain known as Imari was first fired in Japan around 1660
and soon showed up in palaces across Europe.

By Ann E. Berman Produced by Doris Athineos

Left: An Imari bowl
and stand with gilt
bronze dolphin
mounts. The
porcelain was fired
in Japan, circa 172
and mounted in
France, circa 1740
Imari was placed
on a pedestal in
princely palaces.

FUNCTIONAL MASTERPIECE

At Casablanca, quality and sophistication never go out of style. That's why each fan is created with only the highest grade of materials and the most meticulous craftsmanship, to ensure a lifetime of quiet, reliable, energy-efficient performance. Whatever your taste may be, you'll agree that your Casablanca fan is a work of art.

CASABLANCA®
WORLD'S FINEST CEILING FAN

CHINESE Imari plate	JAPANESE Imari plate
Circa 1720	Circa 1690s
Lighter porcelain body	Heavy porcelain body
Red overglaze brighter and more translucent than Japanese	Blue underglaze darker than Chinese
No spur marks; sometimes foot rim slightly browned	Spur marks in foot rim
Worth about $10,000	Worth about $8,000

SAY "IMARI," AND IMMEDIATELY A PICTURE of the l
liantly colored red, blue, and gold porcelain seen at every antiq
show in America comes to mind. Although named after the Jap
ese port town Imari, the densely patterned porcelain was made
both Japan and China beginning in the 17th century, and beca
so popular that porcelain factories in Germany, France, and E
land copied the palette and patterns. From rare, historical por
lains to decorative, inexpensive accent pieces, Imari still draw
crowd more than 300 years after it was first invented.

THE JAPANESE GET INTO THE ACT

Imari production began in the mid-17th century, before E
peans learned how to make porcelain and still depended on Ch
for their supply. About 1650, political unrest in China sudde
halted porcelain production, and the Dutch East India Com
ny—the only Western entity then allowed to trade with Japa
turned to the porcelain kilns at Arita in southern Japan.

The wares produced there incorporated Chinese and Japan
motifs (chrysanthemums, plum blossoms, birds, pine trees, fa
etc) and were often decorated with a distinctive blue undergla
applied before the piece was glazed and fired, and overglaze po
chrome enamels, applied after the initial firing. The result
more colorful than Chinese wares—it could even rival Ita
maiolica—and soon large quantities were being shipped from
nearby port of Imari, giving the porcelain its now familiar na
(It's also still known as "Arita ware.") By the time China got its

Continued on page 76

Top: Porcelain room at Charlottenburg Palace in Berlin. Chinese and
Japanese porcelains were mixed together without regard to origin.

PHOTOGRAPHS: TOP—CHARLOTTENBURG PALACE/BERLIN, SPSG; JAPANESE PLATE—SEATTLE ART MUSEUM/PAUL MAC
CHINESE PLATE—PRIVATE COLLECTION/FORMERLY RALPH M. CHAIT GALLE

lements of tile create the space.

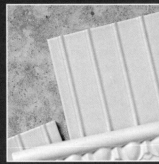

Compose the room of your dreams. Choose from
an array of beautiful tiles and colors
~exclusively from these dealers of
Pratt and Larson tile.

PRATT & LARSON

together again, Japanese porcelain had become so popular that it continued to be exported to Holland and, via Chinese traders, to other European counties. This trade continued until Europeans learned to make their own porcelain in the mid-18th century, a development that virtually dried up Imari imports.

THE SECOND ACT

A hundred years later, Imari was back in business. Commodore Matthew Perry, an American, engineered a treaty with Japan in 1854 that opened up trade to England, France, and America. Lavish displays of Japanese porcelain began making a splash at international fairs like the 1876 Centennial Exposition in Philadelphia. The richly patterned, brighter, more decorative pieces made in 19th-century Arita appealed greatly to Victorian America, which imported them in large numbers. Toward the end of the century, new producers like the Koransha and Fukagawa factories opened, making ever more elaborate and distinctive pieces. Some of these factories are still in business.

EARLY vs. LATE: THE GREAT MARKET DIVIDE

The market for Imari is as divided as these two eras of production. Collectors who prefer 17th- and 18th-century pieces turn their noses up at anything later than 1800, while buyers who look for the more decorative 19th-century pieces eschew earlier examples, finding them too plain and cerebral. Accordingly, many dealers specialize in one era or the other. Auctionwise, Sotheby's and Christie's offer only early pieces in their main salesrooms. The nineteenth-century Imari is offered at their bargain salesrooms in London and New York and at smaller auction venues all around the country.

In the early period (1660 to 1800), the term 'Imari' is more specific, referring only to one of several types of porcelain shipped from the port of the same name. "There are two important styles produced during this era—Kakiemon and Imari," explains Jeffrey Olson, an Asian specialist at Christie's. Kakiemon pieces have a white body sparsely decorated in a distinctive palette of overglazes in salmon, turquoise, pale green, cobalt, and yellow enamels. The Imari palette features the distinctive blue underglaze finished with overglaze enamels in white, red, gold, and sometimes green—often with black outlines. Other early styles include

The Japanese call Imari "brocade-ware" or *nishiki-de*, based on the many motifs taken from richly patterned fabrics.

pieces with European armorial designs, "Chinese" b[l]ue-and-white patterning, and molded figures and anima[ls].

Who buys? London dealer Daphne Rankin finds [that] "early pieces tend to go back to Japan or to American[s or] Europeans doing an English-country-house look. T[hey] like big jars to set on hall tables or garnitures for m[an]tel pieces." Condition is more or less important, depe[nd]ing on what side of the pond you are on: "Americ[ans] want their pieces absolutely perfect," says Ran[kin,] "while Europeans don't mind a few rivets." (Often in[vis]ible, metal rivets or staples were used to reassemble b[ro]ken porcelain.) Prices vary greatly. An extremely [rare] late 17th-century Kakiemon figure of a horse rece[ntly] brought $875,000 at Sotheby's, but prices for more o[rdi]nary pieces usually sell at auction beginning at $2,00[0.]

Later Imari (1800–1920), although a continuation [of] the 18th-century Imari palette and decoration, beca[me] more densely patterned as the century progressed. Americans [are] the biggest buyers. "American collectors love it," says Jean Scha[lk] of New York's Flying Cranes Antiques. "They tell me: 'I feel a[live] when I see it.'" Luckily, seeing it is no problem: Every antiq[ue] shop in the country can boast a piece or two—in a dazzling arra[y]

Continued on page 78

Top: An Imari vase, circa 1710, sits on an English gilt console table at Knole House, England. **Above:** Imari figure of a woman, circa 1690. Figures of humans and animals were popular with the European aristocracy.

Shoes are *Definitely* overrated.

There's something about Mohawk carpeting that begs to be touched. Maybe it's the superior quality. Perhaps it's our craftsmanship. One thing's certain, bring home a Mohawk carpet and you may never want to put your shoes on again. Call 1-800-2-MOHAWK or visit mohawkind.com.

Aladdin | Horizon | World | Galaxy | WundaWeve | Portico

MOHAWK®
Mohawk makes the room

Innovations Collection, Rodeo Drive

shapes, from teacups to giant palace urns. Chargers, decorative forms (like fish plates), and pairs of vases top most collectors' wish lists. At leading dealers, the best examples are in the $1,000-to-$8,000 range. But slip down a notch or two in quality, and you can find mid-19th-century plates for $150 to $200 apiece. Late-19th-century pieces made by the Fukagawa workshop, on the other hand, are always at the top of the price pyramid. Intricately patterned, almost modern-looking, important pieces of Fukagawa can top $40,000.

THE DATING GAME

Dating Imari is more of an art than a science. Although some pieces are marked on the foot, these Oriental characters are notoriously unreliable: "The Japanese used to put Chinese marks on Imari pieces to make them look like they came from China," laughs Rankin, the London dealer. The signatures on later pieces like Fukagawa are more useful. Learn to recognize them, and you'll know what you've got. Likewise, if a piece says "Made in Japan," it was probably made after 1911. Since similar Imari-type patterns were used for centuries, a piece so decorated could have been made in 1670 or 1870. Use your eyes and hands to figure out which. The heavier the porcelain and the denser and more elaborate the design, the later such a piece is likely to be. Another hint: Schaefer suggests inspecting the gilding. A gently worn look means the piece has some age to it.

WHICH PERIOD OF IMARI SHOULD YOU BUY?

The answer depends on your taste and motivation. For investment, most agree with James Marinaccio of New York's Naga Antiques, who believes that, because of their historical importance and rarity, "earlier pieces will be worth more in the long run." Such pieces may also be a good buy just at the moment: "It's definitely an opportunity," says Sachiko Hori, vice president of Sotheby's Japanese department. "Because of their economy, the Japanese are not buying, and there are not a lot of new American collectors for Imari."

THAT OTHER IMARI

Don't be surprised if a dealer offers you a piece of Chinese Imari. When the Chinese kilns reopened in the late 17th century, porcelainmakers discovered that the Japanese style had caught on with their European clients. So they began to make their own Imari-style porcelains—stopping when interest petered out about 1760. Today, prices are about the same for both, but the collecting population differs. Most buyers of Chin[ese] Imari also collect other Chinese—not Japanese—export porcelain. One who collects o[nly] Chinese Imari, Benjamin Franklin Edwards III of St. Louis, has found that "experts often [dis]agree on whether a piece is Chinese or Japanese."

Continued on page 80

Above: A group o[f] Japanese export porcelain vessels, including Imari an[d] Kakiemon wares. Imari was commo[nly] copied by the Chinese. **Left:** This Chinese Imari plat[e] circa 1750, was on[ce] owned by Paul Revere. It's now on display at the Peabody Essex Museum.

IMARI TIME LINE

1660	1680	1689	1700s	1708
Red-, blue-, and gold-colored Imari porcelain made in the port town of Arita, Japan, sets sail for Holland.	Chinese copy Imari colors and designs but add new shapes.	Louis XIV melts down his table silver in order to replace it with porcelain.	Imari becomes the pet porcelain of European aristocracy.	Germans discover how to make porcelain; the Meissen factory imita[tes] the three-color Imari palette and patterns.

DDEN
LENTS
RE
NGER
DDEN
TO THE HOME DEPOT
HR
EMIUM
US
E
LORS
AT
AKE
E
OM

ssive colors
-picked by
tional Home
Behr paint,
sively at
Home Depot.

INTERIOR
AI-GLOSS ENAMEL

BEHR
REMIUM
PLUS.
Lifetime Guarantee

Ultimate Durability!

A PURE WHITE

First In Home Improvement℠

homedepot.com

THE
HOME
DEPOT

DEFINING STYLE Continued from page 78

Here are a few clues: "Chinese porcelain is thinner, and the clay body is finer," explains William Sargent, curator of Asian export art at the Peabody Essex Museum in Salem, Massachusetts. "Hold it up to the light. If it's translucent, it's probably Chinese." Christie's Marley Rabstenek says that Japanese Imari designs are "less dense, more spread out" than the Chinese versions and suggests checking for spur marks within the rim of the foot. "Only the Japanese set pieces on blocks in the kiln," he says. "When those blocks were broken off after firing, they left a pattern."

PORCELAIN PALACES

From the 1680s to the 1740s, Imari was the hot dish in grand European houses. Entire rooms were organized around Oriental porcelain collections displayed on brackets, shelves, mantels, tables, and specially designed pyramidal étagères, often against mirrors that reflected their patterns and colors into infinity.

Perhaps the most elaborate example was the Schloss Charlottenburg, built in the early 18th century in Berlin by Elector Frederick William of Brandenburg for his wife Sophie-Charlotte. Its porcelain room was a festival of specially designed surfaces, both horizontal and vertical, on which was displayed an immense collection of Oriental porcelains—from huge covered urns to tiny dangling bottles—artfully arranged to produce an aesthetic whole.

Right: Chinese Imari lidded jar, circa 1700, with French gilt-bronze mounts, circa 1745.

ENGLISH Imari plate

- Chelsea factory, circa 1756

- Soft-paste porcelain

- Scalloped rim with 12 panels

- Brocade pattern inspired by Japanese fabric

- Worth about $1,000

JAPANESE Imari plate

- Circa 1720

- Hard-paste porcelain

- Scalloped rim with 16 panels

- Called "brocade-ware" or *nishiki-de*, because of its resemblance to the richly patterned fabric

- Worth $3,000

IMITATION: THE SINCEREST FORM OF FLATTERY

The fad for Imari had a major effect on m 18th-century European porcelain desi When Augustus the Strong of Saxony found his factory at Meissen in 1710—the first Eu pean shop to make hard white porcelain— ordered designers to copy the Imari in his o collection. In the 1730s, the French porcel factories at St. Cloud and Chantilly follow suit. England's Queen Mary was also an Im fan, and soon the Bow, Chelsea, Worces Derby (and later the Spode) factories w turning out their own versions. The Imari st became so ubiquitous that people forgot Oriental origins and began to think of it sim as "18th-century."

WHERE TO SEE IT

The Peabody Essex Museum in Salem, Mas chusetts, has one of the world's most comp hensive collections of Asian Export art and ow an Imari plate that once belonged to silversm and Revolutionary War patriot Paul Revere.

For more information, see the Reader's Resource on page 188.

1750	1828	1837	1854	1876
In England, first Chelsea, then Bow, Derby, and Worcester copy Imari motifs.	Great fire in Arita halts Imari production.	Tiffany & Company is founded.	Imari revival occurs after Japan agrees to open trade.	Philadelphia exhibiti sparks interest in Oriental porcelain.

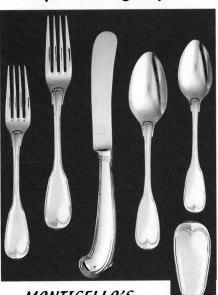

AIRPORT FOOD
PRALINES A "CHEWIE" CANDY WORTH YOUR CARRY-ON BAG

We used to think we hated airport food, but that was before the American food revolution found its way to our in-transit oases. Today, delicious, often regional, foods can be worth carrying home for a special gift or just for your own enjoyment. These unusual pralines, *right,* filled with Texas-size, still-crunchy pecans, are chewy and addictive. They're made by the Lammes Candy Company of Austin, Texas, which has been in business for 100-plus years. Call 800/252-1885, or get in touch at www.lammes.com. The candy is shown on Annieglass footed glass slabs; 888/761-0050.

TRENDS
A CEVICHE TRIO

Popular in Latin America, ceviche is seafood "cooked" by marinating it in citrus (usually lime) juice, which firms the flesh and turns it opaque. Chef Jason Segal serves a scrumptious three-part ceviche sampler at L.A.'s Mojo restaurant, known for its ambience, gorgeous celebrities and delicious food. Prepare ceviche with the freshest seafood available. We blanched our scallops, shrimp, and fish for 30 seconds to kill surface bacteria, marinated them in lime juice, then added a salsa-like mixture. The shrimp version included tomato, orange, and lime juices. For coconut ceviche, try red snapper, halibut, sea bass, or tuna with lime juice, coconut milk, and fresh ginger. Adapted from Chef Segal's repertoire, these are a special treat, especially served in Mexican glasses, as we did for a recent summer fiesta.

SCALLOP CEVICH

- **2 cups fresh bay scallops (abo 1 pound)**
- **1½ cups lime juice**
- **½ cup chopped tomato**
- **2 tablespoons chopped onion**
- **2 tablespoons snipped fresh cilantro**
- **1 serrano chili pepper, seeded and finely chopped**
- **1 tablespoon olive oil**
- **¼ teaspoon sugar**
- **¼ teaspoon salt**

Immerse scallops in boiling w for 30 seconds. Drain. Sprea even layer in shallow baking Add lime juice to cover. Cover chill overnight. Drain scallops discard lime juice. Place scallop medium bowl. Add tomato, on cilantro, serrano pepper, olive sugar, and salt. Stir gently to c bine. Cover and chill 1 to 4 h to develop flavors. Makes 2 cup 8 to 10 appetizer servings.

Continued on page 84

PHOTOGRAPHER: PETER KRUMHA

Pfresh Pfavorite.

Putting a pfresh new pface on your kitchen? Start with our Savannah™ pfaucet. Its classic styling and pfine porcelain handles make it the perfect pfit with any decor. As for pfeatures, you'll appreciate Savannah's high-arching spout that accommodates large cookware. Plus, its broad reach covers every inch of the sink. Each one is also backed by our Pforever Warranty,® which covers both pfinish and pfunction for life. Traditional style meets timeless quality. Now that's a pfresh idea.

TASTE
COOL AND REFRESHING

SUMMER AND WINTER SANGRIA

Sangria in summer and winter versions occupies a place of honor at the elegant Atwood Cafe bar in the renovated Euro-style Hotel Burnham in Chicago's booming Loop. Red and white wines form the basis of the wine, liquor, and fruit drink. Culinary-school graduate and bar manager Michael Doerfler incorporates seasonal fruit, brandy, and a chef's trick of allowing the drink's ingredients to blend flavors and "mellow," for days before serving. Both summer and winter versions include seasonal fruits. The drinks' rich jewel tones are reflected in the massive bar mirror that also shows the crowd of beautifully garnished imbibers.

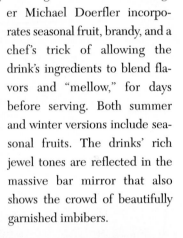

Bar manager Michael Doerfler with his signature sangria drinks at the Hotel Burnham in Chicago's Loop.

MASTER RECIPE
Use 1 liter of red and1 liter of white wine, preferably burgundy and chablis, plus ¾ cup sugar. In winter, add such seasonal fruit as pears, apples, and citrus slices, plus cognac or brandy to taste.

SUMMER SANGRIA
Start with master recipe ingredients, then add 1 cup each of gin and Cointreau. Before serving, add summer berries and such seasonal fruit as cherries, peaches, apricots, and plums.

TOOLS
OF THE TRADE

CHEFS CAN'T LIVE WITHOUT

The Convenient Spider When you need to cook more than one kind of food in a large amount of water, don't bother using a fresh pot for each. Instead, skim cooked food out of the pot with a spider—not the cast-iron skillet this word often describes, but a large, flat strainer, **right**—and reuse the already-hot water. From Bridge Kitchenware, where spiders come in three quality levels: Asian-style bamboo and metal; chromed steel; and all stainless steel. The midpriced chromed-steel tool is lighter than the stainless, but it must be dried thoroughly to avoid rusting. Available in sizes ranging from 5 to 9 inches in diameter for $5.95 to $9.95; call 800/274-3435. In New York, call 212/838-1901.

> Cooking is like love. It should be entered into with abandon or not at all.
> —HARRIET VAN HORNE, NEWSPAPER COLUMNIST AND POLITICAL PUNDIT

Continued on page 86

PHOTOGRAPHER: LEFT, PETER WALTERS; RIGHT, GREG SCHEIDEMANN

Color
coordinate
your
life

Amtico

800-291-9885
www.amtico.com

Works of Art You Can Walk On.
™

EVERYTHING OLD IS NEW AGAIN

Sweet onions, like the ones shown here, are higher in sugar, which not only gives them a sweeter flavor but helps them caramelize better. And they're especially delicious when thin-sliced raw for sandwiches.

All onions start somewhat sweet, developing a stronger, more pungent flavor as they age. Therefore, locally grown onions, picked in summer to last the entire year, are, by definition, no longer sweet once they're not fresh from the onion patch. The special so-called "sweet" onions—Vidalias, Walla Wallas, and a few Texas varieties—formerly available only during a relatively short season, now can be found year-round. They are imported from Mexico and Central and South America during the off-season in the United States, allowing American supermarkets to cater to our appetite for these delicious bulbs the entire 12 months of the year. Lucky us!

LIFE WAS **GRAND** ON MY COCONUT ISLAND,
BUT THIS IS **DOUBLE** THE DELIGHT.

NOW **COOL** CREAM SOARS TO PEAKS OF PERFECTION.

BURIED BY A **FRESH**, JUICY AVALANCHE,
I AM UNDISCOVERED TREASURE.

KITCHEN LIBRARY

Two Chefs Who Are *Not Afraid of Flavor*

Chefs Karen and Ben Barker met on their first day in cooking school. They both wanted to own and operate their own restaurant, and soon they decided to pursue their goals as a husband-and-wife chef team. Seven years, several restaurant moves, and one child later, they opened the doors of the Magnolia Grill in Durham, North Carolina, bringing with them their professional training and experience, a wall full of awards, and a conscious Southern sensibility. "We serve down-home food, but with a twist," says Ben. Their recipe for osso buco, for example, calls for pork shanks and is served with Creole Baked Beans. They prepare grits, but in a cheese-enriched soufflé. And their idea for a rich Butterscotch Sauce includes America's favorite, bourbon whiskey. Shown, *above right*, with macerated Georgia peaches, it's a dish that's as spirited as the chefs. Their new cookbook, *Not Afraid of Flavor* (University of North Carolina Press; $29.95), is perfect for those who love regional food.

BOURBON BUTTERSCOTCH SAUCE

1½ cups whipping cream	1 teaspoon vanilla
1½ cups sugar	½ teaspoon lemon juice
5 tablespoons unsalted butter	2 to 3 tablespoons bourbon

Heat cream over medium heat just to boiling. Remove from heat. Place sugar in large skillet or heavy saucepan and heat over medium-high heat until sugar begins to melt, shaking skillet occasionally to heat sugar evenly. Reduce heat to low; cook until sugar is melted and golden brown, about 5 more minutes. Stir as necessary after sugar begins to melt. Carefully add hot cream to caramelized sugar. (Mixture will spatter and steam.) Cook and stir about 1 minute more to dissolve sugar lumps. Remove from heat.

Stir in butter, vanilla, lemon juice, and bourbon. Cool and serve warm or at room temperature over ice cream, cake, or fruit. (Sauce can be covered and chilled for several days. Reheat before serving.) Makes about 2 cups sauce.

CLASSICS REFRESHED

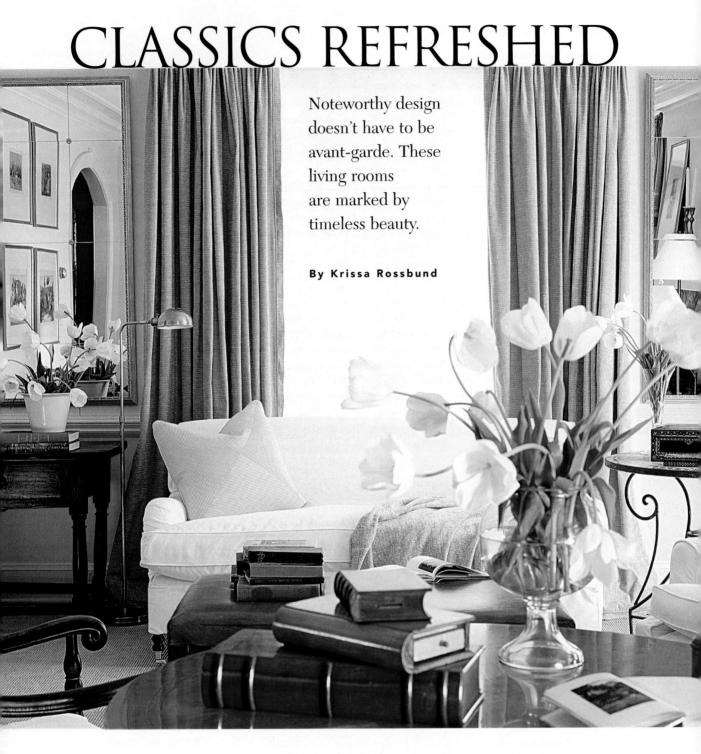

Noteworthy design doesn't have to be avant-garde. These living rooms are marked by timeless beauty.

By Krissa Rossbund

TRENDS ARE WHAT CATCH OUR ATTENTION and keep our creativity fresh a moving. Be it a car with a space-age look, a hip pair of jeans in shiny red leather, or a sle chair made of colored Lucite, innovation inspires us and makes us come back for mo But sometimes the best aesthetic is the presence of classics that withstand the test of tin simply offering beauty and comfort.

Interior designer Ron Cacciola created a perfect example of an understated room lovely that one forgets whether it's classic or contemporary, cutting-edge or traditional love rooms that are timeless," says Cacciola of his family room in the New Caanan Sho

Continued on page 90

PHOTOGRAPHER: TRIA GIO
REGIONAL EDITOR: BONNIE MAHA

Red.
Love at first sight.

The object of this room is not to knock out or assault with design.

—INTERIOR DESIGNER RON CACCIOLA

SHOWHOUSE SHOWCASE Continued from page 88 house in New Caanan, Connecticut. "The object of this room is not to knock out or assault with design."

A simple color scheme launched the room's uncomplicated decor. Citron yellow walls meld so gently with taupes and ivories in the fabrics that the room has a monochromatic feel; the furnishings marry lights and darks seamlessly. The traditional English sofa and chairs avoid stuffiness with casual slipcovers in a brushed white denim. The only exception to the slipcovered seating is a reproduction spool chair upholstered in paisley. Custom mirrors, each divided into multiple panes linked together with pewter buttons, flank the windows, dressed with soft taupe sheers.

An interesting collection of tables—a leather-top cocktail table, a round Duncan Phyfe reproduction, an iron Moroccan piece with a tile top, and an antique walnut side table—give the calm room some shots of surprise.

Continued on page 92

SHOWHOUSE SHOWCASE Continued from page 90

INTERIOR DESIGNERS LOVE A GOOD CHALLENGE ev
now and then, but a room with spectacular architecture like t
stately oval parlor at the Boston Junior League Showhouse
Massachusetts offers special delights.

"A parlor, by definition, is a room set aside for the enterta
ment of guests," says interior designer Wendy Reynolds. "I wan
the design, especially the colors, to be for the evening—sparkl
and promoting great conversation."

The trick for Reynolds was to balance the existing classi
framework with casually elegant furnishings that provided a co
fortable and relaxing gathering spot. Inspired by the lavend
raspberry, ivory, and beige colors of the linen floral she chose
the sofa and lounge chair, Reynolds covered the walls in a str
raspberry. Moldings and wainscoting are painted in beige
white, respectively, subtle enough to create fool-the-eye shade
rather than giving the look of two different colors.

The real surprise is in the fireplace surround and mantel. Wl
layers of old paint were removed, black glass panels set into a c:
iron frame were discovered. The glass panels had originally b
"reverse painted"—a technique in which decorations are done
the back side of the glass and then viewed from the front of
pane—to resemble marble.

The seating area blends a nice mix of casual fabrics—the strip
linen floral, a tone-on-tone chenille, flame stitch, and damask—
in ivory. The Egyptian Oriental rug, chosen for its mellow and a
appearance, offers a smart contrast to the intense walls.

Continued on page 94

PHOTOGRAPHER: ERIC R
REGIONAL EDITOR: ESTELLE BOND GURAL

a new showcase for premium auctions

Traditional auctions, contemporary style. Over the years, your style has certainly changed. And now, the way you buy fine and authentic antiques, furniture and accessories will change too. At eBay Premier™ you can browse, bid on and purchase the things you desire in a safe, enjoyable online auction environment. All from the place where you show your style—your home. **www.ebaypremier.com**

eBay Premier™

The Art World's Online Marketplace.

> The soothing blue was fitting in this summerhouse that sits on the water.
>
> —INTERIOR DESIGNER KIM BARRETT

SHOWHOUSE SHOWCASE Continued from page 92

WHAT'S NOT TO LOVE about the hallmark color combination of blue and white? R
dered on fine Chinese porcelain or as a document toile, it is crisp and sings of cool c
trasts to hot summer days. That was the approach of interior designer Kim Barrett wl
she delivered the restful color palette to this living room at the Duxbury Historic Soci
Showhouse in the seaside community of Duxbury, Massachusetts.

"I wanted this room to be historically nautical, like a sea captain's room," says Barr
who determined that soothing blue and white plus antique furnishings were fitting in
200-year-old house on the water. Wing and Martha Washington chairs and a camelback s
were given a fresh lift with blue-and-white cotton toile slipcovers. A contemporary glass-
iron cocktail table serves the seating area, and a walnut table with Delft tile inserts sh
off new blue-and-white ginger jars. The color scheme continues at the windows, wh
French-pleated, blue-and-white checked silk draperies hang from fluted poles be
dentil molding. The walls were painted white, then striéd with a blue glaze to add a bi
texture. An old painting of sailing ships above the mantel carries out the nautical theme

For more information, see the Reader's Resource on page 188.

PHOTOGRAPH

homelife®

real life. real style.

GET A GRIP AND STOP GRIPING

How to complain effectively and save yourself aggravation in the process.

By James V. O'Connor

There's always the danger that a complaint from a diner may result in a cosmic payback in the kitchen.

WHEN SALLY RAN INTO A COUPLE OF FRIENDS at the supermarket, they started grumbling about the new principal at their kids' school. "The principal had announced some outrageous new rules, and in talking about her and her rules, we became rather vehement," recalls Sally. As they grew noisier and louder, someone finally told them they were blocking the aisle. That someone turned out to be the principal's husband.

Let's face it, complaining can get out of hand. Of course, we all have reasons to complain—legitimate causes to gripe. We have every right to protest when we want to correct an injustice, failure, or bad decision. The challenge is to deliver our grievances so that we sound civilized—and achieve our goals.

Conversational complaining involves sharing displeasure or venting with friends, family members, or co-workers. If the topic is a stressful job, noisy neighbor, or rebellious teenagers, we might be either seeking advice or looking for sympathy. A caveat: When the problem is unsolvable, as in complaining about dreary weather or endless traffic, it can be boring and annoying, labeling you as boring and annoying, too.

Remember the adage about flies being attracted to honey, not vinegar? There's no doubt that complaining with civility and retaining a sense of humor can help resolve your problem. And, hey, wasn't that the point of complaining in the first place? At work, for example, the boss says, "You're the most productive worker in this department, and I know I can rely on you to handle this new project."

You thank her for the compliment even though you are tempted to speak your mind: "The best worker? Could it be because I stay late every night and work at home on weekends? And if I'm such a good worker, why did I get a measly 3 percent raise this year? Save the sweet talk. Show me the cash!"

Of course you could derive satisfaction, even pleasure, from such a tirade. But, let's face it—you could also damage your relationship with your boss with your sour grapes.

So how *should* you register a workplace complaint?

Don't respond to appreciation with a complaint. And never complain impetuously. Decide exactly what you want to say and how to phrase it. Take time to craft a convincing memo that lays out your dissatisfaction and proposes solutions. At the very least, your written thoughts will help you organize what you want to say.

Continued on page 98

What Do You Call A Work Of Art That Can Save Up To 40% On Home Energy Costs?

Vista® 20531

A Hunter Ceiling Fan.

Saving Money Never Looked This Good

Tired of skyrocketing energy costs? Well, here's some good news: Using a Hunter ceiling fan can help you save up to 40% on your summer cooling bills and as much as 10% on winter heating costs.* What's more, styles ranging from turn-of-the-century traditional to state-of-the-art contemporary make Hunter fans the most beautiful way to save! And every whisper-quiet Hunter fan is backed by a lifetime limited motor warranty. That's guaranteed peace of mind from the company that invented the ceiling fan back in 1886.

AirMax®: The Power Of Efficiency

Hunter fans are powered by our advanced AirMax® motor.** Its patented construction features an internal impeller and cast aluminum rotor, making it the coolest, most efficient Hunter motor ever.

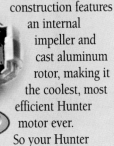

So your Hunter fan will move more air more efficiently, without sacrificing quiet performance.

Get Set To Save Even More

Want to save even more? Install an easy-to-use Hunter programmable thermostat! Hunter thermostats feature state-of-the-art technology that can

help you save up to 33% on home cooling and heating costs. And even the most advanced ENERGY STAR® model can be do-it-yourself installed in under 30 minutes.

For more information on the complete line of Hunter fans and thermostats, or to find the dealer nearest you, call 1-800-4HUNTER or visit us online.

QUIET FOR LIFE

www.hunterfan.com

ETIQUETTE Continued from page 96

How you complain is also importan
home. You and your mate have pledge
spend a lifetime together, and tact and di
macy are essential.

Say you sit down for dinner and hate
meal. The new recipe looks like pond s
and has the consistency of gravel. What to
Jack, a friend who always seems to know
to be gracious, advises giving the coo
in his case, his wife—credit for trying,
admits that when he cooks, he doesn't v
criticism either.

His wife, Annie, explains. "He'll say so
thing like, 'The meat's a little chewy, but
seasoning is perfect.' "

Surprisingly, Jack is not the same perso
a restaurant. Annie says he examines everyth
on the plate before the waiter walks away,
doesn't hesitate to send it back. "He's very f
about food when he's paying for it," she s
"and he's made a few embarrassing scenes."

Annie has worked in a restaurant kitc
and believes this is a major risk. The thou
of what might be done to his food back in
kitchen makes her laugh. She thinks th
could be a cosmic payback for being diffic

Jack, on the other hand, thinks he's d
restaurants a favor by telling them w
wrong with the food and how to fix the p
lem so that future customers will be satisf

And it's true that approaching some
who can fix whatever is upsetting you is so
times necessary. But there are tactful way
do it. Let's say you're overcharged for a
chase on a credit card bill. If a simple
doesn't work, write a formal letter, explai
the situation briefly and in businesslike
guage. Attach copies of all necessary rece
canceled checks, etc.

If your complaint goes unanswered, ma
follow-up telephone call within 14 days. N
the time to find an individual who can h
not a recorded message. Explain that
have written a letter and offer to fax a copy
sure to get the name of the person you sp
to. Be extra-polite, since those who wor
customer service are used to being mistre
and will surely respond better to politen
That's not to say you should be a pusho
Be persistent. Be definite. Be clear ab
what you want.

The least effective and most annoying k
of complaining is heard from the chronic c
plainer. Admit it, you don't want to listen,
neither does anyone else. By constantly fo
ing on what is wrong or foolish, this compl
er not only ruins the day for others but can
himself or herself into a very bad mood.

"I have served customers who are ne
satisfied," says Laurel, a sales associate
department store. "They're furious whe
don't have the dress they want. They req

Continued on page 100

THERE'S A CHANCE OF FLOODING IN YOUR AREA. ARE YOU WILLING TO BET THE HOUSE ON IT?

Well, are you? You'd be surprised at how many homeowners are still willing to risk everything they have over a small insurance premium.

The sad fact is that floods are a nightmare not just experienced by "other people." In too many cases, we don't have flood insurance because we make the mistake of believing our homeowners' insurance covers flood damage. It doesn't.

Yet, for little more than $100 a year, depending on where you live and the coverage you choose, you can get National Flood Insurance. That's hardly a lot for the peace of mind that comes with knowing you can depend on a policy that's backed by the Federal Government.

What's more, National Flood Insurance is easy to get through your own insurance agent.

Don't take a chance. Make the call.

CALL NOW-1 888 724 6789
(TDD# 1 800 427 5593) or
talk to your insurance agent.
www.floodalert.fema.gov

FEMA's National Flood Insurance Program-
working with Project Impact to build
disaster resistant communities. PROJECT IMPACT

BE FLOOD ALERT

NATIONAL FLOOD INSURANCE PROGRAM

ETIQUETTE Continued from page 98

constant attention, and if they have to wait, they become very demanding."

But having said this, Laurel quickly adds that she is making an observation, not complaining.

"My job is to make these people happy. I move fast. I call to see if what they want is available from another store in our chain. I recommend alternatives. Sometimes it works, and then sometimes nothing will satisfy a customer. I know they're unhappy people, and I try to feel sorry for them rather than angry."

Chronic complainers aside, not all of us want to stop complaining. Our egos may not allow us to tolerate difficult people and situations. We may have attention spans that are too short, very little impulse control, and thus have a low tolerance for anything we see as troublesome.

But as modern life becomes ever more demanding and stressful, the need for patience and tolerance becomes greater.

The next time you feel you are the victim of an injustice or an indignity, give some rational thought to the situation before you complain or, heaven help us, make a scene.

Here are some ways to make complaining more useful and satisfying for everyone involved.

Control your emotions. It's worth the struggle. There's no doubt that people are more willing to help if your complaint is justified and if you present it in a calm, mature manner. No one likes being yelled at, even if they're wrong. If you fly off the handle before you have clearly assessed the situation, the one who is embarrassed and apologetic may be you.

Accept the fact that things go wrong and that people make mistakes. You will be understandably upset if an usher seats you in the wrong place and you have to move when the ticket holders show up. When someone disconnects you when transferring your call, it can be annoying.

But everyone goofs once in a while, so soften your anger with a little compassion. The airline lost your luggage? What can possibly be gained by creating a scene? The luggage claim adjustor didn't create your problem and he or she

will be far less willing to help if you t[r]y make the situation yet more difficult.

Carefully consider the realities of [the] situation. The sales clerk might be new [or] incompetent. If the restaurant is crow[ded] and you see your waiter working hard [and] moving fast, try to be patient. If your f[light] is delayed because of bad weather, or [the] problem is mechanical, be grateful yo[u're] not up in the air!

Make certain you're not part of [the] problem. Hate waiting in lines? Be ob[ser]vant. At the post office, you may need t[o fill] out a form for some services before you [get] to the window. Busy delicatessens and [bak]eries often req[uire] customers to ta[ke a] number. If the [line] at the movie [box] office is long, [per]haps you sho[uld] have left home [ear]lier in anticipa[tion] of the crowd. Be[tter] yet, try to go [to] crowded event[s at] "off times," wh[ich,] by the way, [are] worth discoveri[ng].

Get the fa[cts.] Your son says o[ther] kids were pickin[g on] him, and the teacher didn't stop them. [Be] supportive, but ask your son to be ho[nest] about *why* they were picking on him, [and] where the teacher was at the time. Get [the] teacher's side of the story. As much as [we] like to believe them, our little darlings [are] not always innocent victims. Always ga[ther] as much information and documentatio[n as] you can before you complain.

Help out. No, you can't write your [own] airline ticket when the line is long, [but] when the supermarket cashier is bag[ging] groceries, the line is long, and you're [in a] hurry, you can help. And when all you n[eed] is a clean fork at a busy restaurant, you [may] be able to easily find one yourself.

Try to see humor in the situation. [This] may be the best advice of all when c[om]plaining. So many acts of incompetence [are] truly laughable. The best humor is base[d on] human mistakes and foibles. So w[hen] you've survived an incident and h[ave] calmed down, laugh as you relate y[our] tale of woe to friends. They'll be m[ore] appreciative if you entertain rather t[han] complain. And you know what? You'll [feel] better, too. ▦

James V. O'Connor is the author of a b[ook,] Cuss Control, *and last wrote for* Tradit[ion]al Home *on how and why to swear [or not] swearing. He lives in Northbrook, Illino[is.]*

> When you've survived an unpleasant incident and have calmed down, laugh as you relate your tale of woe to friends.

Dinner's ready

Stouffer's Family Style Favorites

Enjoy

How do you get the whole family

around the table?

Stouffer's Family Style Favorites

Macaroni and Cheese.

Tender macaroni in a creamy

sauce made with two kinds of

cheddar cheese. A taste hungry

sea monsters find irresistible.

Stouffer's

Nothing Comes Closer to Home.
www.Stouffers.com

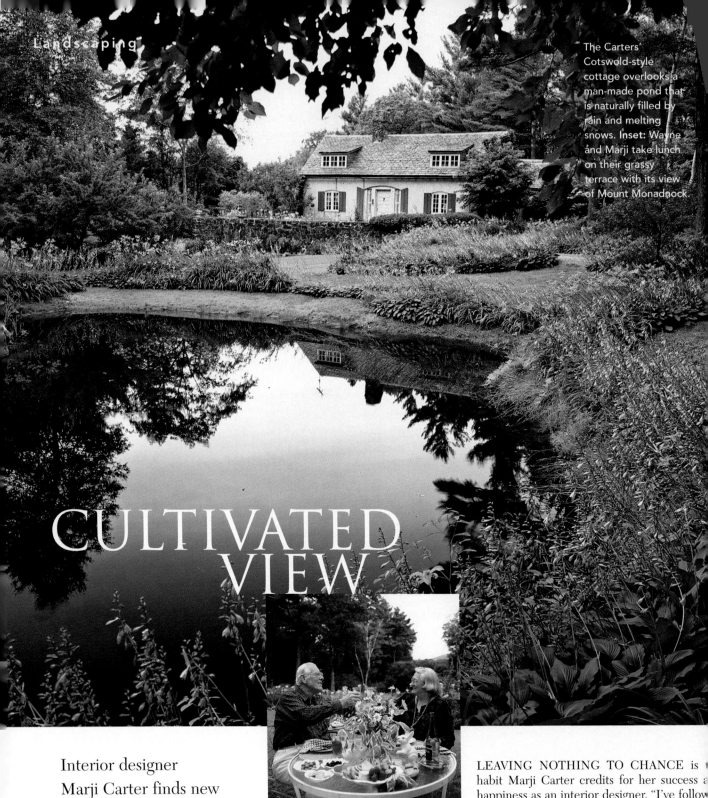

The Carters' Cotswold-style cottage overlooks a man-made pond that is naturally filled by rain and melting snows. Inset: Wayne and Marji take lunch on their grassy terrace with its view of Mount Monadnock.

CULTIVATED VIEW

Interior designer Marji Carter finds new freedom working by the acre instead of by the yard in her New Hampshire gardens.

By Elvin McDonald

LEAVING NOTHING TO CHANCE is habit Marji Carter credits for her success happiness as an interior designer. "I've follow the same policy with my gardens," she says, despite over 20 years of moving the earth in order to create a he enly place, Marji still maintains, "Everything in life is a gift."

When Wayne Carter's profession first brought the couple New England from Texas by way of California, they looked at "interesting properties" throughout the region. Blueberry named for its plethora of native blueberries on 65 acres of N Hampshire countryside, was the 301st. "Technically, the house Cotswold-style cottage with Italian Renaissance features," M explains as she reveals its status on the National Historic Regis It was designed by Joseph Everett Chandler, a Boston archit

Continued on page 104

PHOTOGRAPHER: RICHARD FE

LANDSCAPING Continued from page 102

and dean of Harvard University's School of Architectur
and completed in 1932 as a summer cottage. Except f
its windows and ironwork, the cottage was constructed
materials that were cut and carved right on the proper

If location is at the top of the desirability list, th
good bones must come next. "Chandler also laid out t
formal garden in 1936," Marji says, "and we've kept tr
to his vision for everything within the wall confines a
terraces." Following sound principles of design, t
architect extended the rectilinear lines of the house i
the immediately surrounding outdoor spaces. Ma
with Wayne's constant encouragement, has dared to

beyond, to take off into the w
blue yonder, represented by ac
of hilly woodland, rocky terra
and views waiting to be carved
of the vegetation. Here the nat
al curves of the land—and so
she has imposed—serve as t
inspiration for sinuous beds
hardy perennial flowers and bu
shrubs, shade trees, and conifer

"I didn't understand garde
ing," Marji says, "but as a desigr
I understood line and color. Sis
Parrish always said, 'Make roo
where people feel comfortab
and I believe the same prem
applies to garden rooms. At
very beginning, Wayne and
asked ourselves what would p
vide comfort for us and for
guests." As it turned out, the qu
tion had several answers.

"We added a cutting garden
interior bouquets, a vegetable g
den for good, fresh food
herbs, a terrace from which
watch the sunsets, and a pond
a cool oasis. We've been carefu
preserve the woodland betw
the house and the road, for pr
cy and the proper setting for
enchanted cottage."

Left: Marji has painstakingly trained English ivy as a living frame for the arched entry into the kitchen, the first door visitors see. The flagstone walkway provides sure footing without being intrusive in the country setting.

Below: A stone birdbath sits on the wall below the back terrace. The bay window at left, filled with flowering plants, is where Marji has positioned the kitchen dining area. "I'm view-conscious," she says.
Right: An elevated bluestone terrace at the back of the house overlooks the original gardens. The latticed concrete pot on top of the wall and the planter boxes were chosen by the architect.

With her energies focused on creating comfort, M
set out to learn about the local climate and what per
nials and bulbs might be expected to thrive in this p
of short summers and long, seriously cold winters.

"I asked questions at the local nursery, did a lo
reading, and added to the plantings bit by bit," she s
"Designers are fortunate, because we can turn a vi
into a reality."

The pond, with its view to Mount Monadnock, of
dramatic proof of Marji's visualization talents. Sitec
front of and somewhat lower than the house, the p
replaced boggy ground where wild blueberries o
grew with abandon. The ease with which this appare
natural basin of water rests in the landscape is a te
ment to the will of a woman with a dream and of a
with a backhoe and a bulldozer. That man in this ca
Richard Cumings, a neighbor Marji describes as
landscape sculptor, who is a whiz at working with he

Continued on page 106

Left: The view from the terrace to Mount Monadnock on the distant horizon, was created by Marji's removal trees and vegetation that blocked the sight line, now emphasized by towering birches th were left standing. The pond that replaced a blueber bog adds interest the near distance.
Below: An antique bench with griffins favorite design mo of Marji's, invites a rest to contemplat the pond and surrounding plantings of hosta and daylilies in cool pinks and pale yellows.

LANDSCAPING Continued from page 104

equipment." He also moves rocks and helps transplant trees and shrubs. Beyond the pond, large trees had to be removed in order to open up the view. "I had some grave doubts along the way as first one tree and then another had to go," Marji confesses, "but as Mount Monadnock began to be revealed, Wayne and I were both filled with joy."

Encouraged by that success in carving out a view, Marji says: "I found the courage to remove a few more smaller trees that were obscuring some towering native birches. I love the verticality and silvery whiteness of the trunks. They are like exclamation points in response to the glory of the mountain and vegetation as far as the eye can see."

The gardens feature tulips, dogwoods, and forget-me-nots in spring, which doesn't arrive in New Hampshire until May. The flowering dogwoods are planted in a rocky bed. "I was told that this variety wouldn't flower here, at an altitude that is 500 feet too high and 50 miles too far north," Marji says. "But in gardening as in decorating, there are times when it pays to be adventurous and break the rules."

June spills over with peonies and rhododendrons, followed in the summer by lilies, hostas, and daylilies. "I keep dated maps and notations of my gardens; they enable me to appreciate the progress. With-

Continued on page 108

How to Survive Stressful Home Renovations

Chapter 9
Dust: Living with the Enemy

You vowed at the beginning of the project to be overly aware of its dreaded existence. Yet still, through it all, dust managed to find its way onto every available surface in the house. Relax, you have fallen upon information you can actually use. First, buy yourself those little paper booties. They look ridiculous, but they won't track dust throughout the house. Be sure someone (nobody said you) vacuums a bit every day. It hasn't been scientifically proven, but dust seems to multiply on its own, usually at night. And finally, put a box fan in the window, blowing out. Dust will fly in the direction of the fan and then scoot harmlessly out of the house. And by all means, choose CertainTeed building products. Your contractor, who is already sold on the stuff, will love you. And that goes for whether you're doing an addition or building a Victorian, Colonial, Cape or any other style. What's more, you'll love the fact that CertainTeed products are virtually maintenance-free. And that an amazingly thorough amount of attention was paid to detail and quality. Which, in the end, makes the dust that's created worth the effort.

Try these stress relief options

Roofing & Ventilation

Siding

Insulation

Fencing & Decking

Windows

Choosing CertainTeed building products means you care about style, durability and comfort. And with our SureStart™ warranty coverage, which includes both labor and material costs,* you also have peace of mind. Call 1-800-782-8777 or visit **www.certainteed.com**

CertainTeed ⊟

Quality made certain.
Satisfaction guaranteed.™

*See actual warranties for specific details and limitations. © CertainTeed Corporation 2001

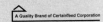
A Quality Brand of CertainTeed Corporation

Left: What started 20 year ago as three clumps of dayl and five hostas has multiplied into thousands flowers. "All I was dig and divide," Marji says. "Nature the rest."

LANDSCAPING Continued from page 106

out this record, even I wouldn't believe that this all started with three clumps of daylilies and five hostas twenty years ago. All I've done was dig and divide and let nature do the rest."

Marji has also had the restraint to plant only the flowers that thrive in her gardens and that she loves most. Instead of a little of many things, she has planted drifts of a few flowers. "The flowers of all the same hosta encircling the pond are my lavender lace. I don't think so much about the individual blossoms but rather the effect of thousands and thousands—well, I'm from Texas," she says with a hearty laugh. The orange daylilies have adapted so vigorously that unknowing visitors often mistake them for native wildflowers. 'Connecticut King' lily, a tall, yellow true lily, is one of Marji's favorites. "Their glow draws me into the

garden, and they have good, long stems making big, generous bouquets."

Marji herself does most of the main nance. "I'm an early riser," she says, "an plant, deadhead, and weed at least th hours a day, two days a week. I focus on foot at a time. When I was a child, mother was an avid gardener, but couldn't even get me to water with any r ularity. Now my five thousand daylilies tended as if they were my children.

After two decades, Marji says she is c tent to refine and adjust the plantin "always striving for the best views and p spectives from our favorite spots.

"I feel richly blessed," she adds. "Wl all is said and done, the gardens my sanity."

Regional editor: Estelle Bond Guralnick

Left: Marji designed the gate, an anniversary gift from Wayne, "t keep the puppi in but not bloc the view." Fron the entrance, a glimpse of the front terrace offers a graciou invitation.

n a shopping spree at The Home Depot and you'll get the cart for free.

Grand Prize: A new Toyota Tundra, $5,000 in Home Depot merchandise and a consultation on a home decorating/remodeling project with a design expert.

Enter at bhg.com/winatruckloadofstuff

TOYOTA

Q&A

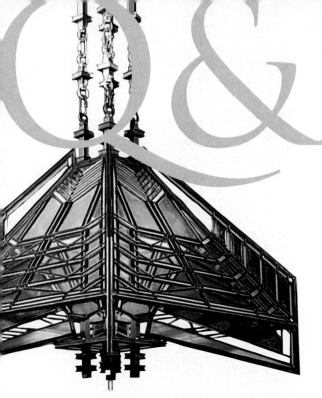

Get great solutions to your decorating problem from today's top design experts by e-mailing those tough questions to *Traditional Home*.

Produced by Krissa Rossbund

We are building a home using house plans that have been modified from original 1902 plans. We want to keep the structure as historically and architecturally accurate as possible. The exterior is stucco and brick, has a tile roof, and is designed in a mixture of Prairie School and Italianate architecture. What type of lighting fixtures should we consider for the formal sections (entry, parlor, and dining areas) of the house?

Lynn K. Green
Ridgeland, Mississippi

Chicago interior designer **TONY STAVISH** thinks the simple design of the Prairie School Arts and Crafts style would suit your formal spaces best. "The parlor and living-room chandeliers should relate to each other, but not match.

The metal finish should be pewter or dark antique brass. Avoid any kind of high-gloss or lacquered finish. The Oakland table lamp, *right*, made of copper and mica, is from Rejuvenation Hardware ($333; 888/401-1900). The suspended light, *top*, designed by Frank Lloyd Wright in 1902, is featured in *Living in the Arts and Crafts Style* (Chronicle Books, 2001), a decorating workbook featuring furniture, lighting, and patterns appropriate for this style.

What do you put in two wall niches that are arched and have a spiral pillar separating them? The living room niches are the first thing you see upon entering the front door, and are approximately 36x18 inches. I like traditional, but eclectic things.

Paige Elliott
Dallas, Texas

Because of their positions, artist SA SHANNON-DAILEY recommends treating niches as one unit. You really have sev options, depending on the style you prefer

One option is to paint or wallpaper back wall of each niche with a color that trasts with the shelves. This will offset niches from the rest of the room, highligh the objects you plan to showcase. Col glass in various shapes would look spectac against a solid-colored wall.

Another idea—hire an artist to paint a orative scene on the back walls of the niche pastoral landscape scene would create effect of a window view. The outer edge the niches could be painted to give the loo a stone or brick arched window frame.

Continued on page 112

ILLUSTRATOR: THOMAS ROSBOR

NOW <u>ALL</u> OUR PRODUCTS COME EQUIPPED
WITH A BUILT-IN VOTE OF CONFIDENCE.

LIMITED WARRANTY TO CONSUMERS
★
Good Housekeeping
Promises
REPLACEMENT OR REFUND IF DEFECTIVE

s if you didn't have enough confidence in our products, all new Lennox equipment is covered by the Good Housekeeping
al. If a product bearing the seal proves to be defective within two years of purchase, Good Housekeeping will replace
e product or refund the purchase price. For complete details, see your local Lennox Dealer or call **1-800-9-LENNOX**
visit **www.lennox.com.**

HEATING **LENNOX**® COOLING

ONE LESS THING TO WORRY ABOUT.®

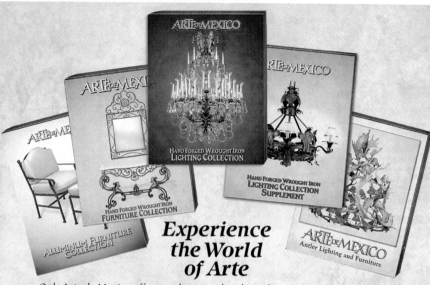

We are building a Caribbean-style hou͏ Florida, and we need help with furn͏ arrangement. Our great room measures ͏ feet. Our furniture consists of a 7-foot-long͏ two 5-foot-long love seats, two tall plant st͏ two coffee tables, one round side table, a͏ leather chair.

—*Fred and Dale B͏*
Delray Beach, Fl͏

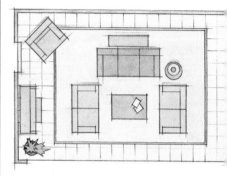

Traditional Home resident interior designer͏ DAVIS notes that with your floor plan, you ca͏ rather flexible in your furniture placement.͏ decide what you want the focal point to be. ͏ you spend a lot of time outside, you could ͏ the outdoors the center of attention.

Place your sofa facing the glass doors, ͏ add the two love seats so they face each oth͏ balance the area. This configuration will allow͏ to use a coffee table in the middle of the ͏ and create angles between the sofa and ͏ seats; the round table will fit nicely in one of ͏ angles. Float your leather chair in a corner t͏ ate another seating area. Adding an ottoma͏ a side table will establish weight in the corn͏ large sisal area rug will tie the furniture toge͏

Our newly decorated living room looks lik͏ old English library. The sofa and two wing c͏ are covered in two different fabrics of v͏ gold. I have accented the room with va͏ black and gold prints on throw pillows an͏ ottoman and love the results. However, wi͏ much gold, I'm at a loss for a wall color͏ baseboards and crown moldings are all stai͏ and there is not much natural light in this sp͏ What wall color should I choose?

Janet Gall͏
Coral Springs, Fl͏

Textiles and furniture designer LILLIAN AU͏ of Boca Raton, Florida, suggests a warm ta͏ your walls. White walls are too extreme ag͏ your rich, gold furniture. To calm the room d͏ advises August, choose a color that is rich͏ neutralizing. This will also play up the richne͏ the stained wood molding. A warm tan ͏ resembles aged leather, such as Benj͏ Moore's Desert Tan or Cork are good choice͏

Continued on page 114

custom rugs!

your size, shape and design –
made in just a few days.

FULL-LENGTH, DOUBLE PANELS COVER TRANSOM WINDOWS

PANELS PUSHED TO BAY EDGES

The easy way to protect beautiful wood from life's bumps and spills.

Now, beautifying and protecting wood is as easy as brushing on Minwax® *Polycrylic®* Protective Finish. *Polycrylic* dries fast and cleans up with soap and water, allowing you to complete projects in less time. And its remarkable clarity and smooth, durable finish let wood's natural beauty shine through. *Polycrylic*, the easy way to keep wood beautiful.

MINWAX®
Makes And Keeps Wood Beautiful®
minwax.com

This Old House
PROUD SPONSOR

I want to update the window treatment my living room, whose dimensions 14x24 feet, and I need some fresh id The fireplace has one window on eit side and is centered on the south-fac wall. The other windows are on the w facing wall in a small, 12-inch-deep bay. problem is that all these windows h beautiful painted 3-inch moldings aro them and have 22-inch-tall, nonopen windows above them. The vaulted ceil starts at 13 feet and stretches up to a s ond story. I really don't like window tr ments, but I think I need them to add sc warmth to the room. Should I cover upper windows or just leave them alo
—*Skip Ta*
Dallas, Te

Nashville, Tennessee interior designer G HINSEN notes that the best way to t your living room windows is to stack length panels at the sides.

Hang curtain panels from rods above transom windows and treat them as unit, from the top of the transoms to floor for all window groupings.

All panels need to be fully operatio so they can be completely opened closed for privacy and light control.

In addition, for the fireplace wall, h two panels on each window rod. Ga panels at outer edges of each window they cover only about five inches of the dow on either side, *top left*.

Another option for fireplace wall: Ha double rod on each of the two wind Stack the fabric panels, one on each sec of the double rods, then push the pane the sides furthest from the fireplace— to the far left, two to the far right.

For the bay window, use one contin rod, and gather drapery panels at the o edges when open, *above*. This design give a sense of symmetry to the overall thetics of the room. ⌂

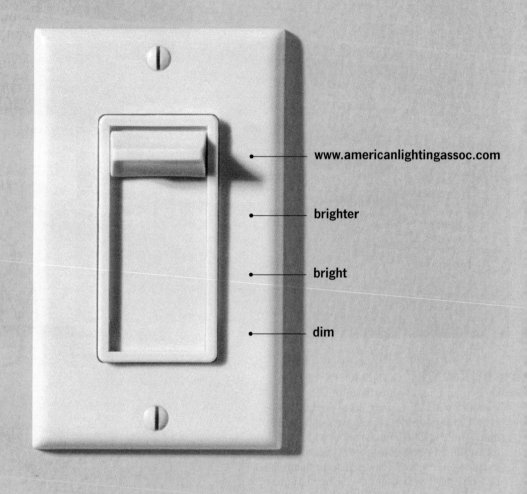

www.americanlightingassoc.com

brighter

bright

dim

THE OFFICIAL WEB SITE OF THE LIGHTING INDUSTRY.

is is beyond bright. Whether you are looking for lighting designs to enhance your home inside or out, the
merican Lighting Association and its members are ready to help at **www.americanlightingassoc.com**.
der informative guidebooks, learn about lighting trends and get tips from professionals, or find an ALA
owroom near you. Visit today or for more information call 1-800-BRIGHT IDEAS.

By playing with
height and depth,
a Chicago
designer remodels
a condo kitchen
without increasing
floor space.

By Eliot Nusbaum

MAKING ROOM IN A SMALL KITCHEN

THE KEY TO MAKING JOHN LEASE'S kitchen and home office fit into such a small space—about 126 square feet—in his circa-1926 Chicago condominium was communication. Well, OK, communication and careful measuring. "We went through every single detail together," says John of his working relationship with kitchen designer Cheryl Hamilton. "There wasn't anything I didn't personally look at and pick out. I knew the materials, the kind of look I was going for, and how much space I needed, and Cheryl took it from there."

Where she took it was to new and different heights and widths. Knowing she couldn't increase the footprint of the room, she did a Jacques Cousteau-like exploration of the depths of the space, fishing for whatever room she could find. And she found a lot. So much that she was able to open up the kitchen, varying cabinet heights and depths to create tremendous visual excitement in a very tight configuration. "In a smaller space, you have to play a lot of tricks with the eye," says Hamilton. "Using a lot of 'steps' in the design helps. This way, the eye doesn't focus on a lot of horizontal lines but is drawn up and down all the

Continued on page 118

Above: By "stepping" the cabinets, designer Cheryl Hamilton broke the horizontal and vertical planes of John Lease's kitchen to minimize the feeling of a very small area.
Top left: In addition to cooking functions, Hamilton found room for a desk for John as well.

misty falls. babbling brooks. whiter whites.

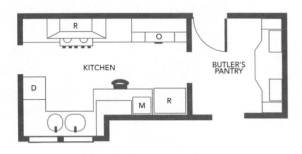

Right: Glass helps reduce the visual volume of the hood over the range. The location of both were dictated by the pre-existing vent pipe, which at least allowed Hamilton to center the two pieces on one wall of the kitchen. The mosaic design on the floor helps define space. **Below:** Among the tricks the designer used to take advantage of all available space was this pull-out pantry, which allows John to easily see and reach supplies.

To fit a smart, functional kitchen in such a small space, communication between owner and designer was critical.

KITCHENS Continued from page 116

time, minimizing the feeling of a small area. want all of the storage and function, yet the de should be clean and uncluttered. It's like a puzz get all of the pieces to fit. Every inch is used. I s many hours designing and measuring to achieve solution." She also created visual excitement decorative elements, like mixing shiny- and m glazed tiles both behind the sink and on the flo

In fact, Hamilton was even able to open kitchen up a bit by eliminating some upper cab and adding storage space to the butler's pa Likewise, she got rid of other cupboards and c ed a striking, almost sculptural, element by han pots and pans from metal rails on the wall. even in the pantry, she was able to eliminate s of the existing cabinets by building a bowfront inet with deep drawers in front and pull-out sto on the sides. Another way she gained space— more accurately, the illusion of space—wa remove the doors and enlarge the openings betv the kitchen and the butler's pantry at one end between the kitchen and what had been the m bedroom at the other. "When I mapped out

Continued on page 120

NOTHING SHORT OF BRILLIANCE

Imagine never having to worry about baked-on foods again. Now even cookware comes out sparkling. At the touch of a button, the exclusive Soak & Scour option unleashes a series of penetrating washes that do the work of soaking and scouring for you. And with 15% more room, it'll hold more dishes than any other dishwasher. The dishwasher, redefined by Whirlpool. It's nothing short of brilliance.

TOUGH BAKED-ON FOODS JUST DISAPPEAR

KITCHENS Continued from page 118

kitchen, I took stock of everything John ha[d] we knew where everything was going to and how much space was needed."

The placement of appliances was lar[ge] determined by pre-existing conditions. example, the stove had to be centered o wall near a vent opening. This left room either side of the stove for equal-sized st less-steel worktables with open storage und neath. The shape of the kitchen sugge[st] putting the sink in the "bay," under a wind A desk area with file cabinets is next to the and actually turns the corner into the w[i] space to offer an open shelf for pictures plants—once again showing how space car used effectively without filling it.

"Cheryl is very good at planning a kitc for the person who will be cooking in it. kitchen is beautiful and functional. And I h[ave] plenty of storage and work space for suc[h] small area," says John. ⌖

Kitchen designer: Cheryl Hamilton
Regional editor: Hilary Rose

For more information, see the Reader's Resource on page 188.

You want all of the storage and function, yet the design should be clean and uncluttered.

— KITCHEN DESIGNER CHERYL HAMILTON

Above: The bowfront cabinet in the butler's pantry meant more storage space with fewer units. The center section is used for storing linens; the side cabinets hold bar items and bottles.
Right and far right: Detailing in the butler's pantry includes the mosaic checkerboard in the floor and laminated glass inserts in the upper cabinet doors.

Something tells us you like stainless steel.

Introducing the new Brilliance® Stainless finish from Delta.® Stainless steel is a look a lot of people want in their kitchen. It's sleek. It's modern. And it's incredibly durable. For instance, take our Gourmet® kitchen faucet featuring our new Brilliance Stainless finish. On the outside, it's a beautiful match to your kitchen. On the inside, the stainless-steel valve system ensures years of trouble-free use. Both are brilliantly engineered to last a lifetime. New Brilliance Stainless finish. We think you'll like it. **www.deltafaucet.com**

A Masco Company

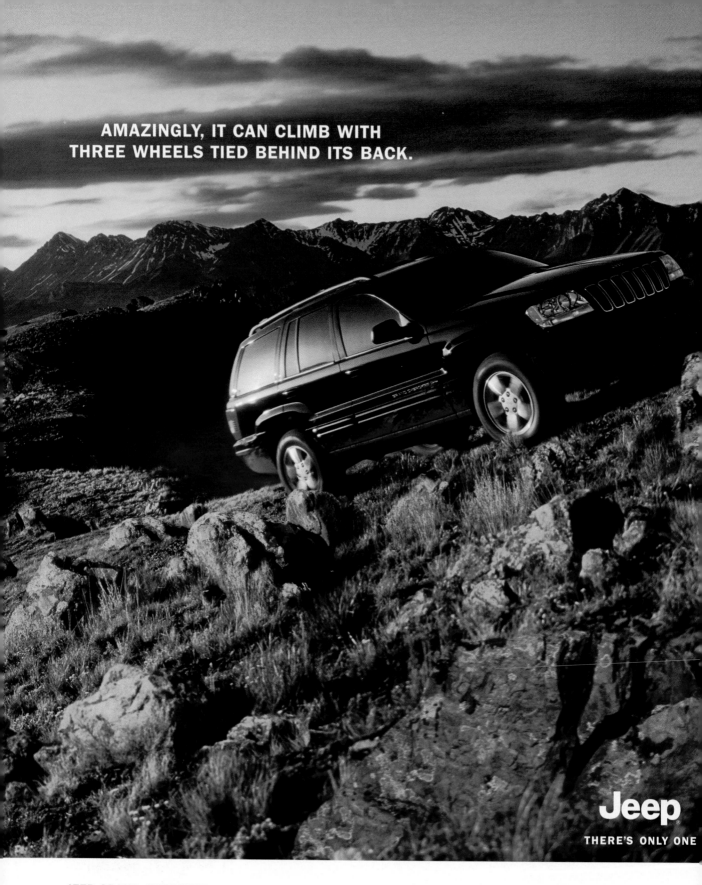

AMAZINGLY, IT CAN CLIMB WITH THREE WHEELS TIED BEHIND ITS BACK.

Jeep
THERE'S ONLY ONE

JEEP GRAND CHEROKEE   It's no ordinary feat. But then Quadra-Drive™* is our most advanced four-wheel drive system ever. This engineering marvel directs power from the wheels that slip to the wheels with traction. So even with only one wheel on solid ground, Grand Cherokee can get you going and keep you going. Amazing—four-wheel drive that's nearly gravity-defying. To get more information, call 1-800-925-JEEP or visit our Web site at www.jeep.com.

*Optional.   Always use seat belts. Remember a backseat is the safest place for children 12 and under. Jeep is a registered trademark of DaimlerChrysler.

THE LITTLE
MANSION

BIG IDEAS AND
GRACIOUS STYLE—
THIS COULD BE
THE START OF
SOMETHING SMALL.

The 17x17-foot living room
makes up most of the first
floor of Sheila Barron's
home. Anchoring the room
is this original brick
fireplace with Georgian
mantel. The painting
above it inspired the
home's interior palette.

BY ELIOT NUSBAUM • PHOTOGRAPHY BY BOB MAUER

Sheila has owned this living room furniture for years, but she had it reupholstered in ivory chenille for a more casual look in her new house. By tilting the oversized French mirror down, she was able to reflect the entire living room. In contrast to the antiques, Sheila chose a contemporary cocktail table, replacing the wood top with acrylic.

THE MAIN DIFFERENCE BETWEEN SHEILA Barron's home and the other mansions on her street in Evanston, Illinois, is the size. Sheila's home is a scant 2,000 square feet. Her "mansion in miniature," as she likes to call it, began life in 1916 as a carriage house tucked way behind a couple of much larger homes. In this former *Traditional Home* Design Award winner's capable hands, however, the modest brick structure is now a beautifully appointed and highly functional Georgian-style home. It proves that well-thought-out plans and attention to detail are far more important than square footage in making a house a great place to live.

"After living in apartments all my life, I wanted a turn at living in a home with property," says Sheila. "When I saw this house, I was taken with the romance of it. It is a small house with a Georgian facade nestled amongst massive three-story Georgian and Colonial mansions. It is set quite a bit back from the street and has about 200 feet of formal gardens in front. In terms of the size of the lot, all I really wanted in the back was a little screened porch or terrace where I could read and have a glass of lemonade. Inside, it was truly a mess, but at that time, I really wanted a wonderful project."

And a project it proved to be for Sheila and her daughter and partner Laura Stoll. "It was apparent when we first saw the house that the remodeling that had been done over the years did not fit the exterior or style of the house," sums up Laura, whose own places

Bottom: The carriage house had two things going for it from the outset: a handsome Georgian brick exterior, and a long approach, which made it possible to plant these inviting gardens. **Below:** Laura Stoll and Sheila Barron.

Right: Sheila maximized the appeal and use of the very small dining area by tucking an antique drop-leaf table and vintage French chairs into a corner by oversized French doors. By closing up an unnecessary exit, she was able to add bookcases for her antique volumes plus a few paintings. **Left:** The stairway was enclosed to make room for this secretary. **Below:** Kitchen cabinets were designed to look like furniture.

have twice been featured in *Traditional Home.* "Inside, it was done like a '50s cottage. Wanting to retain the Georgian integrity of the house, we decided to place a strong emphasis on adding architectural details like the moldings and the French doors."

"At first," says Sheila, "I thought I could just raise the ceilings here and add a little molding there, and it would be a snap. But it turned out it was more cost-effective to gut the house and start over than it was to patch up bad work."

The configuration of the main floor remained basically the same: one large, 17x17-foot living room, a powder room, a small galley kitchen, and small dining area. The biggest structural changes were the removal of a large closet that took away space from the living room; the addition of three sets of French doors along the back of the house; and raising the ceilings—from a substandard 7 feet high in places—by rerouting the plumbing to the upstairs bathrooms.

The all-new kitchen is just 8x8 feet—a size made functional, in part, by moving the refrigerator into the adjoining pantry. Even so, Sheila chose to use only bottom cabinets that she herself designed in the manner of English Chippendale chests to keep them from looking too "kitcheny" when viewed from the other rooms. Next to the

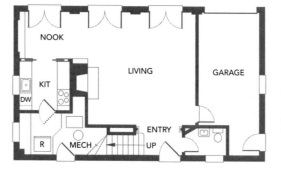

Right: The sitting area at the top of the stairs was created by removing a third bedroom. It serves as both family room and workroom. Sheila describes the Flemish screen above the couch as her most prized possession. **Left:** A local artist painted the Hudson River School–style mural in the powder room. It was both glazed and crackled to get an aged look. Sheila dropped a sink and counter on an Italian gilt console to create the vanity.

MAIN FLOOR

NOOK

LIVING

GARAGE

KIT

DW

ENTRY

R

MECH

UP

SECOND FLOOR

CLOS

BEDROOM

MASTER BEDROOM

WORK/ SITTING AREA

DN

W/D

CLOS

kitchen, is a delightful little dining area that does double duty as a library, with floor-to-ceiling bookcases where once there was a door to the outside. Sheila says she had to have a bookcase somewhere, and placing it here in this corner of the living room helps make the small space feel bigger and more comfortable.

"It's a very cozy area, especially with the antique books I've collected. I had too many paintings for this house, but I couldn't do without those that we've hung on the bookshelves, right on top of the books. I guess it is a little defiant designwise, but we think it is creative, too."

Upstairs, they also had to gut the entire space, reworking the three-bedroom configuration into two bedroom/bathroom suites—one for her and one for Laura's grandmother, who lived with Sheila. The area at the top of the stairs was turned into a loftlike work/sitting area where Sheila sometimes consults with clients. To add volume to this small space, the ceiling was opened through the attic to a height of 12 feet and then finished with a tray ceiling, from which hangs an antique French chandelier.

But what really gives depth and detail to the architecture is the molding. Says Sheila, "One of the highlights of the house is the millwork we put in. We spared no expense with that. We have three-piece, nine-inch moldings throughout the entire house, including the bathrooms and all of the bedrooms. Also, the door

ILLUSTRATION: CARSON ODE

Left and right: Sheila and Laura reversed their color scheme in Sheila's bedroom by bringing in a botanical print with rich greens on a cream background and using pumpkin as a secondary color. Sheila designed the headboard to be tall enough to show above the pillow shams.
Below: Paintings and French pine corbels add character and style to the master bath.

casings are extra-wide, which gives them gusto. We also put in a magnificent railing to the upstairs." In addition, Sheila gold-plated all of the hardware in the house to give it an extra richness and glow.

The home is a triumph not just of substance but of style. "I'm a feeling designer," explains Sheila. "I approach everything by asking how it feels, not how it looks. I examine how I feel when I see something. I try to touch what it does for me emotionally."

For example, Sheila was especially inspired by a 19th-century Hudson River School painting that hangs in the living room. It was the source of the color scheme for the public rooms in the house. "The wall color in the living room came from the painting. We tried yellows and golds, but this acorn squash or pumpkin is the color we kept coming back to. It is just yummy. For me, who's always had an off-white scheme and nothing else, it took a lot of courage to go ahead and do this. It's a big commitment, but I know I won't get tired of it. I feel warm and fuzzy in this house."

And you can bet she'll never feel the walls closing in on her, even if they are within short reach. 🏛

Architect: James Landaker
Regional editor: Sally Mauer

For more information, see the Reader's Resource on page 188.

MARIE AND BILL TRADER CREATED
THE SOUTHERN AND ENGLISH
COUNTRY GARDEN OF THEIR
DREAMS ON A SMALL LOT IN
THE CHICAGO SUBURBS.

BY ELVIN McDONALD

PHOTOGRAPHY
BY RICHARD FELBER

A GEM OF
A GARDEN

Left: The Traders, Bill (holding best pal Nikki, a long-haired dachshund) and Marie (with push-powered reel mower she uses to maintain the lawn), like to spend Saturday mornings in the garden. "Then," says Marie, "we can go play golf." **Below:** Old French wire benches and a wooden butler found in a thrift shop greet visitors at the front door.

Left: The copper frog's-eye view from his "puddle" is to the back of the house, which faces south. All parts of the garden are blessed with at least a half day of sun. Marie favors mostly pink and blue flowers with drifts of white daisies and dianthus that resonate with the white of the house.

"DIAMONDS ARE A GIRL'S BEST FRIEND," says Marie Trader, and then breaks into a big smile as she adds, "but in my case not the kind of diamonds you might think. I love pattern, and when I find one I like, I repeat it. Blue diamonds are painted on the wood floor of my breakfast room, and there are black-and-white marble diamonds in the back entry."

But Marie's diamonds for the patio are a special aesthetic triumph. "I'd seen checkerboards made by alternating blocks with squares of grass," she says, "but I needed surer footing for furniture." She decided on aggregate stepping stones separated by narrow grass strips. "I wanted a big surface that didn't say hardscape and that let you see enough green to look like softscape.

"Salvador Guzman, our yardman, agreed to tackle the project with me. First we put down screening against weeds, then we laid out a pattern of the

Left: To keep the big patio from overwhelming a small space, strips of sod were installed between aggregate blocks in Marie's signature diamond pattern. **Above:** The long bench behind the pond was found at an antiques show in New York. Bill spent his free time one summer building all the garden's lattice fencing.

blocks that we liked. Next, we dug out the screening between the aggregate blocks and wedged in strips of sod cut to fit. I like the grass fairly tall and full, and I keep it trimmed with a small push-powered reel mower."

Having put the carat before the house, so to speak, Marie explains the setting: "When my husband Bill and I first moved here nineteen years ago, the house was all red brick in a sea of overgrown shrubs and trees, which we took out. We removed a porch from the front and built a bigger one. Then we painted it all white and added black shutters and black-and-white awnings."

Next came the front garden, which Marie saw as more orderly and formalized than it had been before. "I wanted the graciousness of Charleston," she says. "We put in a broad, straight walk from the sidewalk to the front door using old salvaged bricks from Philadelphia." They installed new wrought-iron fencing and a gate, designed in a style based on snapshots the Traders had taken of their favorite fences and gates.

Inside the front gate on either side of the walk, Marie added two small, formal rose gardens. In the doing, she learned a lesson that would serve her well when it was time to do the gardens behind the house: "I used a hose to lay out

Right: Although remarkably similar, the birdhouse on t[he] left came from Nantucket, the one on the right from Charleston.

Clockwise from to[p] left: The Traders' favorite place to s[it] in the garden beg[ins] with the two Adirondack chairs. "When I spotted t[he] vintage gate in a shop of treasures," Marie says, "I kne[w it] would be the perf[ect] backdrop to creat[e] the effect of a miniature garden." The black-and-whi[te] striped fabric use[d] for all the cushion[s] echoes that of the awnings on the house. Pink-flowe[r] diascia tops the cherubic pedestal. Black and pale gr[ay] diamonds orname[nt] the deck and step[s]. A ready-made sea[t] arbor proved too small for the spac[e], so Marie engage[d a] carpenter to add [a] larger arch and th[e] latticed back with [an] oval cutout. "The lesson I've learne[d] about outdoor furnishings," she says, "is that they usually need to b[e] bigger than you might think."

ILLUSTRATION: THOMAS ROSSBORO[UGH]

the beds, and every time I went across the street to check the effect, I realized they needed to be bigger," she recalls. "In the end, they became twice the size I first envisioned. Scale in outdoor spaces is not the same as inside a house. Things usually need to be bigger rather than smaller; otherwise they lose their impact. In fact, in a small garden, a structure or object that is too small can have the effect of making the overall space seem even smaller."

Until six years ago, the Traders had done little to develop their backyard other than to maintain a grassy sward of lawn and build a pergola along the garage wall. Then Marie received a surprise from Bill on her birthday in July—a card with a flower on the front that said on the inside, "This entitles you to a garden design by Craig Bergmann." The timing was perfect, allowing them slightly more than a year to be ready for their daughter's wedding.

Bergmann, whose name is synonymous with beautiful gardens, recalls their first meeting: "Marie was well prepared. She told me that her favorite gardens were English and Southern, with lots of boxwood and roses, and that she loved a 'country' or 'grandmother's garden' look. We had fun going through a pile of magazine clippings she'd collected over the years and looking at books with pictures that helped me understand her vision."

The result of their collaboration is a visual paradise, with a diamond pattern as its dominant theme. "It is like one big room with lots of different areas," Bergmann says. "The lattice fencing around the perimeter frames the one large space, and then each area flows into the other without a clear separation. It is harder to design a small garden than a large one. In the smaller garden, every area is constantly in view of the others. Marie and Bill have done a marvelous job filling in the details, adding furnishings and objects."

An espalier of the purple-leaved flowering crab apple 'Royalty' in the Belgian fence pattern on the wall between the garage and the house takes the diamond pattern to new heights. "Cabling was attached to grommets installed in the wall to establish the pattern," Marie explains. "We planted a one-year whip at the base of each diamond, then tied in place any growth that fit the design and pruned off any that didn't. It's been fun to watch it fill

Left and above: The arbor with its canopy of 'William Baffin' roses at one end and grapevines at the other was added along the east wall of the garage at the time the Traders were renovating the house. "When I look at these pictures," Marie says, "I see my daughter standing under those roses in her wedding gown. And I remember how the next day we entertained all our families from the East Coast." **Right:** The gate from the driveway to the back garden had to be heavy to hold the antique French lavabo. The espalier on the wall near the garage is 'Royalty' crab apple.

Left: A bee skep and an old rhubarb forcer bring country charm to a garden that is only miles from downtown Chicago. Marie's color theme is expressed here in white daisies, pink roses, and lavender-blue alliums. **Right and below:** Behind the garage is a formally arranged cutting garden centered by a closely pruned 'Cinderella' crab apple. 'Queen Elizabeth' and 'First Prize' roses grow on the latticed wall. Bill built the window box and rustic potting bench. A French wine-bottle holder gives Marie a place to display her collection of vintage terra-cotta pots.

in, and the care is minimal—just an occasional snip snip and tying in place as needed."

One part of the garden not seen from the deck is a cutting garden behind the garage. Measuring 24x24 feet, it is accessed through a center arch, one of three arches covered with 'New Dawn' roses that serve as a living wall. The cutting garden has two lattice fences topped with birdhouses. Another lattice grid, on the end wall of the garage behind Marie's potting bench, has climbing roses. The walkways are pea graveled, and the four square beds for annual cut flowers are edged with antique fencing.

"I wanted a place to do my potting," Marie says, "and where I could grow flowers to cut for the house without taking them from the main garden." A forsythia bush in the sunniest corner provides branches for forcing. Sweet peas planted in spring against one lattice fence provide bouquets until midsummer. "Although it's intended as a working garden, I find the formalized structure gives it a hopeful feeling, even when the beds are empty," notes Marie.

Since the Traders' first goal in planting the garden was to have it ready for their daughter's wedding, they mainly set out larger rather than smaller specimens. "As ongoing policy," Marie says, "I like perennials, but I always welcome any unexpected empty spaces for the fun of trying different annuals. I never tire of updating the interior of my home, and I find the same is true of my garden. How do you resist all the beautiful new things!" ⊞

Garden designer: Craig Bergmann
Regional editor: Sally Mauer

For more information, see the Reader's Resource on page 188.

To reach the front door, visitors pass through an antique gate at street level, then descend a series of flagstone steps to a lushly planted courtyard. The fretwork stair rail is new. **Right:** With the ceiling raised, and new windows and French doors in place, the living room luxuriates in sparkling light from the ocean. At sunset, the soothing neutral color scheme turns to gold.

BEAUTY
BY THE BEACH

BY HEATHER LOBDELL

PHOTOGRAPHY BY JON JENSEN

THE HOUSE WAS SMALL, TIRED, and badly configured. It had narrow halls, little rooms, and limited access to one of its major virtues—a glorious view of the Pacific Ocean. The windows were small and heavily draped. This, combined with low ceilings, obscured a lovely vista. "There was this incredible jewel to behold just 100 yards beyond these walls," says Cher Beall, interior designer, mother of three, and recent transplant to Southern California from Austin, Texas. "And we wanted to reach out and grab it!"

Cher took care of that. She grabbed hold of the view and so much more, transforming the scrappy 1930s beach house into a storybook abode with a new buttery stucco facade, blue-green shutters, window boxes, and a charming garden gate. "The house did have cozy bones, and I liked that," Cher recalls. "But it desperately needed remodeling. We've now created a flexible family home."

The designer's goals were at once simple and complex: Make the house warm, comfortable, and beautiful, and make it highly functional, so that everyone—husband Ken, teenage daughters Lauren and Danielle, and 4-year-old son Charlie—would feel at home. "Because we had limited space to work with, maximizing each inch of the house mattered," she says.

Cher essentially gutted the 2,200-square-foot house and started anew. She raised rooflines, redefined rooms, changed windows,

Opposite: The new dining area/study features a shapely grasscloth-covered banquette with under-seat storage for seldom-used items. The flanking bookcases are new. A faux-skin piano bench provides a touch of whimsy. **Below:** A book lover, Cher added bookcases to the left of the new fireplace, then, to keep the effect from being overpowering, she hung artwork directly on the shelf moldings.

A neutral
color scheme
throughout
the house
adds to the
sense of
soothing calm.

laid hardwood floors, and installed four new fireplaces. She also added 800 square feet of living space, most of that becoming a second-story master suite with French doors leading out to a balcony with ocean views.

Establishing the right palette was one key to this project's success. "Because we live so close to the beach, choosing colors was actually quite a challenge," Cher says. "We have sunshine, but we also have quite a bit of fog. I needed a palette that would feel warm and cozy on chilly days, but airy and light on sweltering ones." With that in mind, walls throughout the house were painted cream and antiqued with a subtle ochre glaze that introduced not only a cheerful tone but a convincing illusion of age. "I wasn't looking for a memorable effect; I just wanted the walls to seem original to the house," Cher explains. "I didn't want anything to scream, 'new house!'" She complemented the walls with soft white paint on newly vaulted rustic wood ceilings and laid honey-hued oak plank flooring that was gouged and scratched on site for a highly distressed look.

Building on these warm-toned bones, she furnished with natural fabrics in quiet neutrals, liberally sprinkling all rooms—including the sun-soaked living room graced by large new windows, French doors, and an arched transom—with texture, texture, and more texture. "I am a very tactile person," she says. "I was one of those kids who was forever being told, 'Stop touching!'" She likens a room with ample texture to a well-read person. "Both are deeper, more interesting."

Quilted cotton warms rooms on chilly days, while loose linen slipcovers, sea-grass rugs, and raffia upholstery cultivate relaxed all-weather elegance. The emphasis on texture extends to chunky leather-bound books and eclectically framed artwork that casually adorns mantels, bookshelves, and walls, lending personality and charm. The result is a home that feels good whatever the weather and offers something else that is very important—respect for the breathtaking beauty that lies beyond its walls. "When your

Right: The small breakfast area is flanked by a new fireplace and a glass door to a pantry created from the old water-heater closet. **Above left:** The street-level entry is romanced with trellised ivy, new flagstone pavers, and an old wheelbarrow. The gate opens to a staircase that leads down to the front door. **Above:** Cher and Ken Beall, with son Charlie.

The new open-plan kitchen/family room was created from a jumble of minuscule rooms.

Left: The new kitchen features pretty cream cabinetry and an island made to look old-fashioned by a chest tucked up against it. Cher saved cabinet space and added interest by hanging her pots and pans. **Above:** Small though it is, the family room seems much bigger now that it opens up to an outdoor living area, complete with an oversized fireplace. The huge finials in front of the fireplace are from an old Mississippi plantation.

oundings are very beautiful, a simplified interior palette is
ys the smartest strategy," Cher points out. "Why try to
pete with the majesty of the Pacific Ocean? It's futile."
eeping window treatments simple is part of this non-
petitive policy. Cher's window treatments do provide light
rol and a softness that romances the beauty of the interiors,
the linen Roman shades and panels here are designed to fade
y, never interfering with the views.
since almost all of the added square footage went into the new
nd-story master suite, space planning in the common areas of
house had to be extra-savvy. The existing dining area, a small
ve where a desk now sits, was tiny. So Cher carved a stylish new
ng area/study out of part of the living room. "With five people
g in a house this size, I couldn't afford to dedicate an area
y to formal dining," she explains. "I needed something highly
tioning." The new dining area features a curved banquette, a
le table, and new built-in bookcases. In addition to seating 10
dinner, the area is used daily as a homework center by the
ls' daughters, and as a place where Cher can spread out
prints or work on photo albums.
he open kitchen/breakfast area/family room also illustrates
r's space-stretching ability. Though petite, this pretty area lives
e and comfortably because furnishings are scaled precisely and
palette is fresh. She combined a jumble of minuscule rooms,
ding closets, a laundry room, and a hall, to give her family a
e to hang out—to cook, eat informally, watch television, and
y the lushly landscaped courtyard through new French doors.

Right: In daughte[r] Lauren's room, a newly added wind[ow] seat offers a cozy spot for reading. Left: A master at use of "borrowe[d] space," Cher add[s] lights and glass-paned doors to h[er] son's closet to ma[ke] it seem part of th[e] room. Below: A s[mall] carpentry bench used as a place f[or] towel storage and supplies creates a playful edge in Charlie's bath.

What used to be the master bath is now son Charlie's 10x11-foot bedroom.

Enhancing the view is a stately outdoor fireplace that Cher added. Inside, another new fireplace—this one with a raised hearth—nestles up to the breakfast table. The kitchen's focal-point stainless range is actually a space-saver. Having the ovens underneath allowed precious wall space to be used for cabinetry.

The Bealls adore every aspect of their remodeled seaside house, from its glorious views to its cozy window seats to its easygoing open floor plan. "For us, this is a very special family home," says Cher. "It's not a mansion, but it has all the magic we could ever want in its warmth, charm, and detail." 🏠

Regional editor: Andrea Caughey

For more information, see the Reader's Resource on page 188.

MICHIGAN'S

FOR THREE MONTHS OUT OF THE YEAR, 24 FAMILIES GATH

BRIGADOON

OR AN IDYLLIC SUMMER ON A SMALL ISLAND IN GULL LAKE.

Children pretty much have the run of Gull
Island. **Left:** Robert Harding pulls his boat along
the shore in front of Beth and Craig Martin's
house. **Right:** Annaliese DeNooyer gets a push
on an old tire swing from her sister Caroline.

BY ELIOT NUSBAUM · PHOTOGRAPHY BY JON JENSEN

Above: The fieldstone fireplace in the Martins' house is original, but they added the mantel and checkered-tile hearth border. They also added the salvaged French doors to the screened porch, being used by daughter Bridget.

IN THE FIRST WEEK OF JUNE,

all of the summer residents of Gull Island gather around a fire pit to hear each of their children read their worst homework paper of the past school year. They then throw the homework papers into a communal fire, and summer begins on the little island.

"It's a catharsis, a symbolic way of saying, 'We leave all of that behind,' " explains Craig Martin. What they are leaving all of that behind for is the kind of place most people dream of, where 24 families gather every summer as they have for generations to kick back and enjoy themselves, their families, and each other.

"Somebody told me when we bought this place, 'If you can't unwind on this island, you can't unwind anywhere.' And that's true," says Craig. "But it goes beyond [...] It teaches you how to relax. The island stays in your heart. It's so[me-] thing you take with you. I think if you asked any of the kids here, [...] would probably say it is magical."

It may be the island, but it isn't just the island. It's the 24 fam[ilies] that give life to the place. Snipe hunts, talent shows, island olym[...] pancake breakfasts on the beach, an annual pig roast, water ballet,

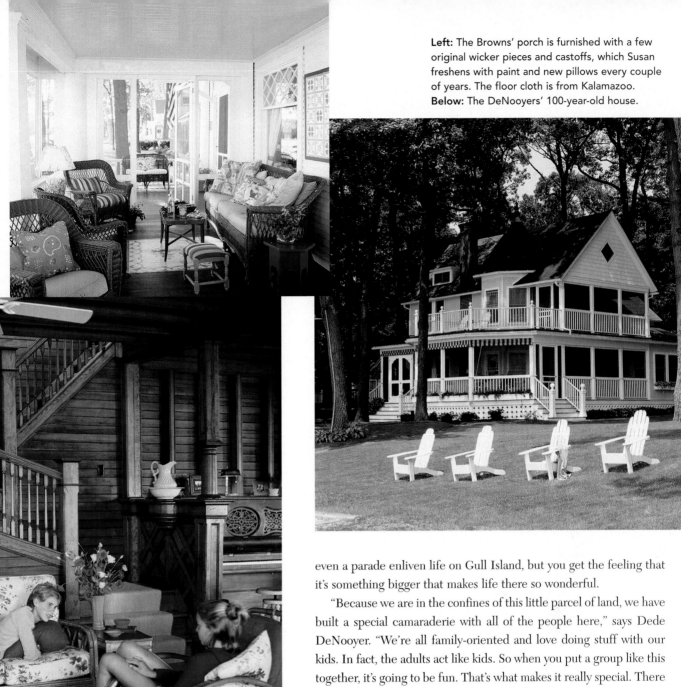

Left: The Browns' porch is furnished with a few original wicker pieces and castoffs, which Susan freshens with paint and new pillows every couple of years. The floor cloth is from Kalamazoo.
Below: The DeNooyers' 100-year-old house.

Above: Sarah and Annaliese DeNooyer chat in the living room of their home, which is in its original state. Much of the furniture is recycled from other homes. The piano is from the old commissary.

even a parade enliven life on Gull Island, but you get the feeling that it's something bigger that makes life there so wonderful.

"Because we are in the confines of this little parcel of land, we have built a special camaraderie with all of the people here," says Dede DeNooyer. "We're all family-oriented and love doing stuff with our kids. In fact, the adults act like kids. So when you put a group like this together, it's going to be fun. That's what makes it really special. There are a lot of beautiful spots all over the world, but if you don't have great people to share it with, it's not the same."

SueEllen Braunlin and Ron Reisman, both of whom are doctors, likewise marvel at the effect of the island and the people on it. Says SueEllen, "There is something special about an island and its isolation. Time marches on everywhere, except on this island. It takes you back in time—it feels like what you wish life had been like when you were a kid. Now we actually get to live it. It is a fantasy; for us, it's just weekends in the summer, but it takes us to a different place and time."

Located about a fifth of the way up Michigan, between Kalamazoo and Battle Creek, Gull Island began life as a church camp in 1907. The island's 24 homes were originally built as cabins, with a common building in the middle of the island where everyone took meals. That building is long gone, and the cabins have been restored and remodeled into charming period summer homes to which kitchens have

SOMEONE ONCE TOLD ME, IF YOU CAN'T UNWIND ON THIS ISLAN

Friends and family gather in front of the Braunlin-Reisman house for a little sun, a bit of gossip, and building sand castles.

N YOU CAN'T UNWIND ANYWHERE. AND THAT'S TRUE. —CRAIG MARTIN

Left: The Browns' living room reflects Susan's love of color. "Color makes me happy, and these colors reflect happiness," she says. "I want you to smile when you walk into my house." She refers to her decorating style as a hodgepodge, but points out how comfortable it feels and looks. **Below:** SueEllen Braunlin and her son, Elias Reisman, share a moment on the porch of their home. The porch had to be completely rebuilt when SueEllen and Ron Reisman bought the house. At that time, they added screens and removed the original awnings to allow more light into the space.

been added. That's not to say folks don't still take meals or just socialize together; they do, but it tends to be a moveable feast, going from home to home to beach to home, and with a changing cast of adults and children.

"Very often, we all get together and have cookouts or dessert together," says Susan Brown. "But some weekends, we just walk around the island at night. We may meet up with somebody and stay up late talking. Everybody just sits on everybody's porch, and you never feel like you are in the way. It's a communal way of living."

That also goes for the kids, who have developed a tradition of hanging out and playing together, regardless of age. "When you're on the island, it's like being in never-never land; I don't have to be grown up when I'm here," says Sarah Martin. "I'm 21, yet I can play with a 5-year-old and have a great time. It's like a perennial camp. It's like growing up with a lot of siblings, and there's always someone to play with."

In fact, it's not unusual to see all of the kids on the island roaming in a pack. "The kids have a great time sleeping together wherever during the summer. They seem to move from house to house, and porch to porch. Sometimes we find 13 or 14 kids sleeping in the guest house behind our home," says Beth Martin. "But, of course, you

Above: It has become something of a tradition that children of all ages hang out together, as here in the Martins' living room. This gathering includes, left to right: Betsy DeNooyer, Caroline DeNooyer, Katie DeNooyer, Teddy Martin, Annaliese DeNooyer, Emily Bauss, and Sarah DeNooyer.
Top right: Susan and Bob Brown's Greek Revival-style house is turn of the century.
Above right: Emily Bauss holds her little sister, Elizabeth, as they swing in the hammock, while the Browns' dog, Coach, takes a nap.

never lose your kids on the island. They can't get off. Unless you hear a boat start up—then you know you're in trouble."

There are times during the summer when the two worlds intersect—for example, when the business people motor over to the mainland in the morning to get to work, or when supplies are needed—and times when the two worlds collide, as on one summer morning a few years ago. As Susan Brown likes to tell it, her husband, Bob, a part-time banker, had to get to the mainland for a very important board meeting: "He couldn't find a motorboat to cross the lake. The boys and their friends had either emptied the gas tank or broken every boat we had. And it was the same with the neighbors—nobody had a boat that was working. So Bob, in his suit, tie, and fancy shoes, had to get into a sailboat at 6:30 in the morning, rig it up, and sail across the lake."

When islanders say it's like extended family, they really mean it, both good and bad. Just like family, you don't really get to choose your neighbors and friends, because the entire population of the island lives within about a quarter of a mile of you. And so you learn to not just live with your neighbors but to see past their foibles to their charms. "You have to learn to live with them as they are," explains SueEllen. "It makes everyone more tolerant and understanding. You are forced to go the extra mile to work things out if you are getting on

Far left: The Browns' kitchen is a playful contrast to the more serious Colonial style of the rest of the house.
Left: The sleeping porch in the DeNooyer home is so popular that family members have to take turns sleeping there.
Right: Alex DeNooyer, Elias Reisman, and Emily Bauss enjoy Gull Lake.
Below: The DeNooyers furnished their contemporary kitchen and the family room with flea-market finds.

each other's nerves. And when I look around, I visualize our kids being friends for the next 60 or 70 years. It influences what we do. I am just as apt to put photos of the neighbor kids around the house as those of my own kids. I think we all have that long-term idea that the cottage will stay in the family."

Eighteen-year-old Bridget Martin maybe expresses it best for all of the generations on the island: "When somebody asks, 'What is your favorite place on earth?' I always say the island. It's not exotic or anything; it's just special." ⌂

Regional editor: Hilary Rose

For more information, see the Reader's Resource on page 188.

Check Mate

An exclusive take on Jim Thompson,
the man who developed the
Thai silk industry, and a first look at
the latest fabric collection.

By Akiko Busch
Produced by Deborah Morant
Photography by Charles Maraia

Places, like people, hav

A slipper chair is dressed in
Patong/Flambeau, an upholstery-weight plaid
inspired by Jim Thompson's 1960s checks—
including the pattern on the pink sheath, **far
right,** which was designed for the author's
mother, his muse. Pillow is made from
Songkla/Heliconia. **Background fabric:**
Singburi/Magenta check. All fabric from Jim
Thompson Thai Silk, 800/262-0336.

heir own style and dress.

Indonesian batiks, Turkish rugs, Navajo wall hangings. In each of these, landscape is as essential to the weave as color and texture. But of such raiments and fabrics, the shimmering silks of Thailand may be the most resplendent.

Certainly, this is what my mother found when she moved to Thailand with my father, then a representative of the Asia Foundation, in the mid-1950s. She was a well-educated, well-read, cultivated American, but all the same, when she went to Thailand, the universe blossomed for her. In part, this had to do with her friendship with a man named Jim Thompson, an American architect, businessman, and collector whose love for Asian art in general and the textiles of Thailand in particular radiated far and wide, from his impact on a single American family to his extraordinary transformation of the textile industry of an entire country.

Today, decades later, the silks produced by his company continue to provide a dazzling festival of checks and plaids, offering their particular luster wherever they appear.

Thompson, trained as an architect and designer, arrived in Thailand in 1945 as a member of the U.S. Office of Strategic Services (OSS), and after the war, he chose to settle in the capital city of Bangkok. Soon he turned his attention to the ancient craft of silk weaving, then a small and faltering folk tradition. He had been drawn to the jewel tones and luxurious textures of the silk since his arrival in Thailand, and he educated himself in the art and craft of its production. Realizing it could best be produced in its native environment, he developed close relationships with the weavers, going from family to family to establish specific colors and patterns that were worked on simple bamboo looms.

His eye for color was precise and imaginative, but he was also a skilled salesman, whether showing his lustrous silks to American visitors or speaking with couturiers and fashion editors on his annual trips to Europe and America. By the mid-'50s, Thompson had transformed a regional folk tradition into a thriving, industry with a worldwide market.

As demand grew, he introduced new, colorfast dyes, foot-operated shuttles, and wider looms, and in the mid-'60s, established a factory in the village of Pak Thong Chai in northwestern Thailand. Located in the country's central silk-producing area, it is a community as much as a factory. Here the mulberry trees are grown and tended, silkworms cultivated, and cocoons reeled for thread.

Thompson was a generous host both to tourists and to Bangkok's resident foreign diplomats, and the charm with which he introduced travelers to his beloved adopted country came naturally. His warmth and graciousness to our family was an example. When he discerned my mother's love of art, he

delighted in advising her as to which porcelains, tapestries bronzes were most worth collecting. And surely he must known that the princess rings—extravagant confections of g piled into conical shapes—that he gave me and my sister whe were very young would remain among our treasured possessic

Thompson's eye for color was legendary, but it was matche my mother's great sense of fashion. While she had assorted ta tional Asian sarongs and stoles made up for her, she also usec Thai silk for full pleated skirts, sundresses, and evening gowr metamorphosis of these familiar Western styles.

Enchantment sometimes travels well, and it came with the when my family returned to America and settled into an house in New York's Hudson Valley in the early '60s. My mo covered an enormous old Chesterfield shimmering blue silk and used gold for curtains, a chaise, and two chairs, burnishing the entire r with Thai light and color and cre an interior landscape that went beyond rural New England.

Jim Thompson vanished afternoon on Easter weekenc 1967 on a holiday in the Cam Highlands in central Mala Speculation continues today a whether he had some fatal dent while walking in the ju was abducted by aborigine was kidnapped by Com nist insurgents. But it is

Using Jim Thompson's new silk collection is an irresistible way to add lighthearted color. **Far left:** Lampshade on bust, Singburi/Pagoda; stacked lampshades, *from top,* Songkla/Blue Harbor; Singburi/Magenta; Songkla/New Leaf; and Singburi/Paradise Green. **On mannequin:** A black/white/gray Thai silk plaid from the 1960s was made into a skirt for Mary Smart Busch, Akiko Busch's mother, shown at **near left** in one of her Thai silk sarongs. The gray plaid was reinterpreted in a large check—Patong/Bangkok Grey—on the tufted sofa, **left,** that the author inherited from her mother. Background plaid is Singburi/Dawn Mist.

timony to his commitment to the Thai people and their arts that the business he established thrives today. A foundation manages his house and art collection, directing proceeds to assorted Thai arts. And the company, now based in Atlanta, Georgia, continues to produce the same lustrous silks he first brought to the market 50 years ago, along with other more contemporary cotton and silk blends and silk/metallic weaves.

The current collection, much of it based on the skirts and sarongs made for my mother in the '50s, includes hues and patterns ranging from the brilliant jewel-toned checks she so loved—lemon, vibrant reds, and hot pinks—to subtler grays and violets. For upholstery, there are also heavier-weight solids—vivid jade, sapphire, turquoise, grape.

And while the family weavers in Pak Thong Chai work much the way they did 30 years ago, contemporary architects and designers continue to use their textiles in innovative ways—for upholstery and curtains, for bed skirts and headboards—because the silks wear well and are incredibly elegant.

Just as my mother's world was forever changed during those years she spent in Thailand, so too does Thai silk carry a resplendent textile tradition to distant corners of the world, transforming other rooms and other places. And for all the myriad ways those shimmering squares of color can be worn, hung, draped, and tied, what they do most elegantly, in my eye, is form a radiant example of the exhilaration that comes when a thing of beauty continues to unfold and reveal itself across generations, landscapes, whole continents. 🏠

For more information, see the Reader's Resource on page 188.

SMALL

PALACES THAT FIT IN A CLOSET, COMPLETE WITH RUNNING WATER AND CUT-CRYSTAL CHANDELIERS

BY DORIS ATHINEOS

The library at Fontainbleau
by model couple Kevin
Mulvany and Susan Rogers.
Opposite: Neoclassical room by
Ron Hubble and Jim Coates.
The Paul Revere sterling silver on
the sideboard was designed by
master silversmith Obadiah Fisher,
a well-known jeweler.

WONDERS

PHOTOGRAPHS: BILL HOLT

Little things matter to Carole Kaye. The founder

of the Museum of Miniatures in Los Angeles rules over a world
where no one is over six inches tall. She owns inch-to-the-foot
replicas of Versailles Palace, Hampton Court, Fontainebleau, and
the Vatican.

"The magic of miniatures is that you create a perfect world,"
says Kaye as she surveys a roomful of surreal estates. "You play
God. It's a wonderful feeling."

In Kaye's mini model homes, tiny clocks tick, and little locks
turn. Cut-glass chandeliers cast a warm glow. A porcelain tea set fits
on a dime. An Aubusson carpet contains 1,600 stitches per square
inch. Mini-tubes of real toothpaste wait to be squeezed. Pop the
cork on a pen-cap-sized wine bottle filled with Montrachet.

Unlike most of the 250,000 miniature collectors in the United
States, Kaye didn't gather only what was already there. She and
husband Barry Kaye, author of *Live Rich*, commissioned artisans to
create dozens of architectural landmarks.

The collection, which is for sale for more than $25 million,
ranges from the ridiculous (a small-scale replica of the Titanic
made from 75,000 toothpicks and two gallons of Elmer's glue)
to the sublime.

Six years ago, Kaye commissioned the British husband-and-wife
team of Kevin Mulvany and Susan Rogers to build a miniature
Hampton Court. "We had to be selective and reproduce only the
most interesting parts," says Rogers by phone from her farmhouse
in West Wiltshire, England. "Otherwise, Hampton Court, on a
scale of one-twelfth, would cover a large swimming pool."

The English Baroque palace miniature is closer to the size of a
coat closet. "Every palace has the same problem when we down-

Left and above: An inch-to-the-foot replica of
the library at Fontainebleau by Susan Rogers
and Kevin Mulvany was commissioned by
collector Carole Kaye. "With large projects,
we have to be selective about the rooms
we re-create," says Rogers. "Otherwise,
we would end up with a replica the size of a
tennis court." For Fontainebleau, the British
husband-and-wife model-makers re-created
nine rooms in the central section. "There
must have been over 100 rooms in the real
palace," Mulvany notes. Their inch-sized real-
estate portfolio includes Versailles, Hampton
Court, and Brighton Pavilion, all constructed
for the Kayes. The cost? Commissioning a
model of your home costs about the same as
buying a flat in central London, says Mulvany.

size it," laments Rogers. At Versailles, for example, "there's an ever-increasing sense of majesty as you get closer to the king. And we have to figure out how to keep that progression going without the same number of rooms."

Details, however, don't disappear. The model couple built Sans Souci for a German collector and furnished it down to the last cup and saucer. "There are over 10,000 individually laid pieces of parquet flooring," points out Rogers, sounding exhausted just from the mere recollection of the Herculean task.

But at least floors are flat. Maine craftsman Harry Smith almost went cross-eyed applying inlay to an undulating bombé shape when he created a palm-sized Louis XV cylinder desk for the Kayes. "Just because it's little doesn't mean I took shortcuts," says Smith, who is paid as much for his miniatures as most furniture-makers earn for full-sized pieces. And why not? The jewel-like desk took fours years to create and required hundreds of drawings as well as a visit to Versailles. It consists of thousands of tiny inlay pieces from 37 kinds of woods, including ebony, satinwood, and holly.

Like Carole Kaye, most miniaturists look to the past for inspiration. Chippendale, Queen Anne, Sheraton, and Hepplewhite are the favorite furniture styles. And authentic details score big points. That means hand-hammered silver teapots the size of a thimble, turned stair rails the width of a toothpick and tiny dovetails. "There's even miniature knitting, using silk thread for yarn and straight pins for knitting needles," says Carol Hardy of the International Guild of Miniature Artisans, a professional society.

Right: Kevin Mul works on a minia of a portion of Hampton Court Palace. The replic was built with 75 individually score bricks. Inside, the parquet floors ar distressed to giv them old-world charm. If there's a knot in the real paneling, Susan Rogers paints on the model in exa the same spot. **Top:** Louis XIII Sa at Fontainebleau The Aubusson ca by Joyce Victorin has 1,600 stitche the square inch. **Left:** Detail of a cabinet in the sal Scale is one inch the foot.

Left: A downsized antique silver shop by Hank Kupjack, master miniaturist. (See "The Master of Minuscule" on page 40.) "He's a real artist," says Carole Kaye. "His realism is very precise. It's mind-boggling."
Right: The marble hall at Sans Souci, the Berlin summer palace of Frederick the Great.
Bottom right: This Louis XV rolltop desk, small enough to fit in the palm of a hand, is by Maine craftsman Harry Smith. It took more than four years to make, incorporates 37 different woods, and is priced at $50,000.

The trend toward realism isn't new. In 1924, Queen Mary, wife of King George V, was given a miniature house with running water and a wine cellar. It's now on display at Windsor Castle.

The Kaye Museum of Miniatures in Los Angeles was scheduled to close at press time, but there are plenty of other mini-meccas around the country. Don't miss the modern San Francisco penthouse, circa 1940, with a real postage-stamp-sized painting by Fernand Léger commissioned by Mrs. James Ward Thorne, on display at the Art Institute of Chicago. The Stettheimer dollhouse at the Museum of the City of New York is filled with tiny artworks by Modernist Marcel Duchamp and sculptor Gaston Lachaise.

Other places to see mini-mansions: The Toy & Miniature Museum in Kansas City, Missouri; the American Museum of Miniatures, Dallas, Texas; and the Tee Ridder Miniature Museum in Rosyln, Long Island. ⋒

For more information, see the Reader's Resource on page 188.

PHOTOGRAPHS: LEFT, E.J. KUPJACK ASSOCIATES; ABOVE, A. KOLESNIKOW

The recipe has been handed down for five generations. Three of which are now sitting at your table.

For years, your grandmother has prepared the perfect Osso Bucco. Tonight, it's your turn. And you have the advantage of a Dacor oven. Our patented Butterfly Bake Element™ cooks traditional recipes with exceptional results. In fact, from now on, everyone gathered at your table may start thinking of it as your special Osso Bucco recipe.

Dacor. Make it part of your family tradition.

dacor®

The life of the kitchen™

girlfriends' weekend

A relaxing getaway is filled with
nourishing talk, joint cooking projects,
and sophisticated comfort food.

BY CARROLL STONER   PHOTOGRAPHY BY ROBERT JACOBS

MENU

DINNER

Champagne with Ribena
Bacon and Cheddar Gougères

Crab Cakes with Spicy Aïoli

Beet and Goat-Cheese Salad
with Spiced Pecans and Green Beans

Spring Lamb Stew in Bread Bowls

Roasted Asparagus

Fresh Pineapple and Dried Cherry
Upside-Down Cake

BREAKFAST

Espresso Granita with Cream
Raspberry and Cream Cheese–Stuffed
French Toast

"WHEN WOMEN FRIENDS get together for a weekend, no matter who they are, the main focus is going to be food and talk," says Chicago chef Gale Gand, who describes herself as a "very good girlfriend." She laughs. "Women are good at taking care of people, and when we're with friends, we like to feed each other, eat, and talk, not necessarily in that order."

"That's it exactly," agrees Deb Kessler, who hosted the gathering photographed on these pages. "Women friends are supportive. And we love to cook for each other, because we have a sense of adventure with food. Getting together with friends feels like a vacation," says the mother of three sons who admits she needs women pals in her life.

What do women eat when they get together? Deb describes her favorite menus as comfort food with a contemporary twist. Gale points out that although women often eat salads at lunch, "when they're together in groups, they order exotic food, love red wine, and seem to like red meat about as much as men."

When Gale created the girlfriends' weekend dinner and breakfast menus, she had several images in mind: One was of the hostess doing some prep work ahead of time so the friends could cook together, but in a leisurely way.

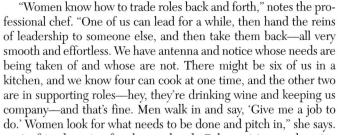

"Women know how to trade roles back and forth," notes the professional chef. "One of us can lead for a while, then hand the reins of leadership to someone else, and then take them back—all very smooth and effortless. We have antenna and notice whose needs are being taken of and whose are not. There might be six of us in a kitchen, and we know four can cook at one time, and the other two are in supporting roles—hey, they're drinking wine and keeping us company—and that's fine. Men walk in and say, 'Give me a job to do.' Women look for what needs to be done and pitch in," she says.

As friends arrive for the weekend, Gale envisions welcoming each with a glass of champagne and something small and delicious. She chose champagne with a drop of Ribena, an English black currant cordial that's a favorite. "Women love champagne," notes Gale, adding, "but then, who doesn't?"

For hors d'oeuvres, she created a recipe for Bacon and Cheddar Gougères. The classic gougère is a puff-pastry ring made with gruyère cheese, but Gale adds layers of flavor with aged American cheddar, two kinds of ground pepper, shredded Parmigiano-Reggiano cheese, Dijon mustard, smoky bacon, and onions.

Besides being moderately easy to cook together, the other requirements for this get-together menu were that the dishes be both sophisticated and comforting. When the group sits down to dinner, for example, the first course is crab cakes with a spicy homemade aïoli, or garlic mayonnaise. These, says Gale, are delicious and easy to make, familiar but impressive "company" food. She also points out, "You don't really need all the ingredients we listed for top-notch crab cakes. They'd be good with fresh, excellent crab, and a little egg white and lemon or mayonnaise, just so they hold together when they're fried." The spiciness of the aïoli, she says, is the perfect touch for diners who like a bold flavor as a counterpoint to the smooth, rich crab.

As the entrée, Gale chose a homey but sophisticated Spring Lamb Stew. The idea came from her childhood memory of eating dinner with her mother at Marshall Field's Walnut Room in Chicago. "Lamb stew came in a little casserole. It was always delicious,

Opening page: For breakfast or dessert—coffee-flavored granita with whipped cream. **Opposite, clockwise from top left:** Champagne with black currant syrup and spicy cheese puffs welcome guests as they arrive. Dinner's first course is crab cakes with garlic mayonnaise. For the main course, chef Gale Gand created a lamb stew served in bread bowls made from a recipe her friend Judy has been baking since she was 11. **This page, clockwise from top left:** "Women listen as well as they talk," says Deb Kessler, *center*, shown with Margaux Engebretsen, *left*, and Lily Handels. "And it's fun to cook for friends, because we're so appreciative." Two friends enjoy a quiet moment during their get-together weekend. A salad has big flavor from ingredients that include beets, green beans, spiced pecans, and goat cheese.

and it made me feel special to have my own individual serving," she recalls. "My mom also used to make me little six-inch pies, and it felt as if she was saying, 'I made this just for you.'" Gale serves the stew in individual hollowed-out bread bowls made from her girlfriend Judy's favorite recipe.

No chef's meal would be complete without a delicious salad, and for the girlfriends' weekend menu, Gale created a Beet and Goat-Cheese Salad, with greens, beets (preferably red and golden beets, when in season), green beans, spiced pecans, and crumbled goat cheese. This medley of flavors blends well and is given even more taste and texture when tossed with an unusual apple-cider vinegar dressing blended with Granny Smith apples, shallots, and walnut oil.

The chef strongly feels that salads, t really good, need lots of compone "Good salads have crunch and layers o vor. If you wish you were eating somet else by the fourth or fifth bite, th something wrong with the salad."

For dessert, Gale's old-fashioned re for upside-down cake is updated with pineapple and dried cherries instead o usual canned pineapple and marasch The fruit is arranged in the traditional amelized brown sugar and butter, w starts out on the bottom of the pan becomes the topping when the cak turned out.

For the next morning's breakfast, Raspberry and Cream Cheese–Stu French Toast continues the theme updated classics. "This combines the of a grilled sandwich and French to notes Gale. "It's crisp on the outside w soft and gooey interior." Smoky cou bacon and coffee are accompaniments

For a final delicious touch, Gale Espresso Granita with Cream. The gr frozen mixture of sugar and coffee is se layered with whipped cream and top with more cream and an orange-peel t

"Coffee time is when you sit aroun table and talk. I need the good, solid of friendship I get from women, and envisioned this meal as small serving many courses, so there's plenty of around the table. This is food to celet with—easy but not effortless to prepar

"It's so natural for women to get tog er around food," adds Deb Kessler. need to connect with other women, food is part of being generous and gi Besides, eating is so much fun!" 🏛

Food stylist: Charles Worthington

Preparation plan and recipes begin on page 1

For more information, see the Reader's Resou on page 188.

Above: French toast stuffed with raspberries and cream cheese and garnished with golden and red raspberries is Chef Gale Gand's updated breakfast version of cream-cheese and jelly sandwiches. **Top:** Gale's new take on an old favorite—upside-down cake made with fresh pineapple and dried cherries. **Right:** Friends toast each other as part of a gathering that combines nourishing talk, cooking projects, and terrific food.

PHOTOGRAPHER: RIGHT, GREG SCHEIDEMANN

This carpet has made it through
countless birthday parties,
two graduation parties,
and a keg party you never knew about.

There's protection. Then there's Scotchgard™ protection. The kind that
helps keep your carpet looking its best longer by making it easier to clean.
So ask for the Scotchgard brand and rest easy knowing the leading name
in protection has you covered. Visit us at www.scotchgard.com

Protection for life's possibilities™

3M *Innovation*

Recipes

Preparation Plan

Although many of these recipes can be prepared ahead, this prep plan is organized so that friends can spend the afternoon before dinner socializing and cooking together.

On your own:
Up to 1 month ahead:
- Prepare dough for gougères; place in freezer container, seal, label, and freeze.
- Prepare Spiced Pecans.

Up to 3 days ahead:
- Prepare Spicy Aïoli.
- Prepare Apple-Walnut Vinaigrette.

Up to 2 days ahead:
- Prepare dough for bread bowls.
- Prepare and freeze Espresso Granita
- Roast beets for Beet and Goat-Cheese Salad; cool, peel, cut up.
- Snap off ends of green beans; blanch beans for salad.
- Peel, core, and slice fresh pineapple for cake.

24 hours ahead:
- Prepare crab cakes; cover and chill.
- Bake bread bowls; store at room temperature overnight.
- Stuff bread slices for French toast; place in covered container and chill.

With friends:
Up to 4 hours ahead:
- Clean greens for salad; dry thoroughly; refrigerate
- Prep ingredients for stew.
- Hollow out bread bowls; cover and set aside.

2½ hours ahead:
- Begin making Fresh Pineapple and Dried Cherry Upside-Down Cake.

1¼ hours ahead:
- Begin making stew.

20 minutes ahead:
- Bake gougères.
- Roast asparagus.

15 minutes ahead:
- Cook crab cakes.
- Arrange salad.

Next morning:
- Dip and bake French toast.

Champagne with Ribena
(Champagne with Black-Currant Cor⌐

Add ribena (English black-currant co⌐ or other fruit-flavored syrup to taste in⌐ vidual champagne glasses. Fill glasses ⌐ favorite champagne.

Bacon and Cheddar Gougè⌐

½ cup water
¼ cup butter
⅛ teaspoon salt
⅛ teaspoon ground black pepper
⅛ teaspoon ground red pepper (opti⌐
½ cup all-purpose flour
2 eggs
⅓ cup shredded cheddar cheese
1 tablespoon finely shredded
    Parmesan cheese
½ teaspoon Dijon-style mustard
¼ teaspoon dry mustard
1 strip bacon, crisp-cooked, drained,
    and crumbled
2 tablespoons finely chopped
    green onions
1 tablespoon butter, melted (optional⌐
¼ teaspoon paprika (optional)

In medium saucepan combine water, ¼⌐ butter, salt, black pepper, and red pe⌐ (if using). Bring to boil. Add flour ⌐ once, stirring vigorously. Cook and stir⌐ mixture forms ball. Remove from heat.⌐ for 10 minutes. Add eggs, one at a ⌐ beating well after each. Stir in che⌐ mustards, bacon, and green onions.

Drop dough into 18 bite-size mo⌐ onto greased baking sheet. Bake in 4⌐ oven for 17 to 20 minutes or until go⌐ brown.* If desired, brush warm puffs ⌐ melted butter and sprinkle with pap⌐ Serve warm. Makes 18.

To make ahead: At this point, puffs ⌐ be cooled and frozen on baking sheet. W⌐ frozen, place in sealed container and fr⌐ up to 1 month. To serve, place frozen ⌐ on ungreased baking sheet and bak⌐ 350°F oven until warm, about 20 minu⌐

Crab Cakes with Spicy Aïo⌐

1 pound lump crab meat, flaked
1 egg
1 egg white
1 small red bell pepper, seeded and ⌐
    finely chopped
2 teaspoons snipped fresh parsley
2 teaspoons snipped fresh cilantro
1 teaspoon lemon juice
½ teaspoon ground cumin

Continued on page 184

ENAISSANCE
AUBUSSON
CARPETS

ATLANTA, GA
Stark Carpet Corp. (To the Trade)
404.266.8959

BOSTON, MA
Steven King Orientals
617.426.3302

CHICAGO, IL
Jorian Rug Co.
312.670.0120

DALLAS, TX
Matt Camron/Hargett Assoc.
214.747.9600

DELRAY BEACH
ABC Carpet and Home
561.279.7777

DENVER, CO
The Rug Source in Denver
303.871.8034

DETROIT, GRAND RAPIDS, MI
Azar's Oriental Rugs
1.800.622.7847

HOUSTON, TX
Houston Oriental Rug Gallery
713.528.2666

JACKSON, MS
Reave's Oriental Rugs
601.362.7707

MEMPHIS, TN
Zaven A. Kish Oriental Rug
Gallery
901.767.7847

NEW HYDE PARK, NY
Data Oriental Rugs & Carpets
516.352.8700

PATTERSON, NJ
Greenbaum Interiors
973.279.3000

PHILADELPHIA, PA
Stark Carpet Corp. (To the Trade)
215.569.1311

LOS ANGELES, CA
Mehraban Oriental Rugs
310.657.4400

For our new to the trade catalog or areas not listed call 800.325.7847.

RENAISSANCE CARPET & TAPESTRIES, INC.
N.Y.D.C. 200 LEXINGTON AVENUE, NEW YORK, NY 10016
PHONE 212.696.0080 FAX 212.696.4248 WWW.RENAISSANCECARPET.COM

Continued from page 182

¼ teaspoon ground red pepper
⅓ cup mayonnaise
⅛ teaspoon kosher salt or salt
⅛ teaspoon freshly ground black pepper
1 tablespoon olive oil

In medium bowl stir together crab meat, egg, egg white, sweet pepper, parsley, cilantro, lemon juice, ground cumin, and ground red pepper until thoroughly mixed. Add mayonnaise, salt, and pepper; mix until well combined.

Form mixture into 12 patties, about 1 inch thick and 2½ inches in diameter. (At this point they may be placed in shallow baking pan, covered, and chilled up to 24 hours.)

Heat oil in large skillet over medium-high heat. Cook crab cakes, half at a time, until golden brown on both sides, 2 to 3 minutes per side. Serve warm with Spicy Aïoli. If desired, serve atop shredded napa cabbage and sliced radishes.

Serves 6 as appetizer (2 crab cakes per serving) or 4 as entree (3 crab cakes per serving).

Spicy Aïoli

1 cup mayonnaise
2 to 4 cloves garlic, minced
2 tablespoons lemon juice
⅛ teaspoon ground red pepper
Dash ground black pepper

Stir together all ingredients in small bowl. Cover and chill up to 3 days. Makes about 1 cup.

Put dollop of aïoli on each crab cake. Sauce is also delicious with other seafood.

Beet and Goat-Cheese Salad
with Spiced Pecans and Green Beans

1¼ pounds red and/or yellow beets
6 ounces green beans
8 cups mixed baby salad greens (mesclun or mixture of such lettuces as red leaf, romaine, endive, radicchio, arugula, frisée, watercress, and/or Boston)
1 recipe Spiced Pecans
1 recipe Apple-Walnut Vinaigrette or ¾ cup of favorite dressing
3 ounces crumbled goat cheese

To roast beets, wrap individually in foil and place in baking pan or dish. Bake in 400°F oven for 1 hour or until tender. Cool, peel, and cut into wedges; set aside. Meanwhile, cook green beans in boiling salted water for 4 minutes or until crisp-tender; drain and place in bowl filled with ice water. Drain again, return to bowl, cover and chill.

In large bowl combine greens, Spiced Pecans, and green beans. Add half of dressing and toss thoroughly. Arrange greens mixture on 6 salad plates. Sprinkle goat cheese over each and arrange beet wedges around greens mixture. Pass remaining dressing. Makes 6 servings.

Spiced Pecans

1 tablespoon brown sugar
¼ teaspoon ground red pepper
¼ teaspoon ground cumin
2 teaspoons walnut oil
1 cup pecan halves

Combine sugar, red pepper, and cumin in medium mixing bowl. Add oil and mix thoroughly. Add pecans and toss until thoroughly coated. Spread pecans out on baking sheet and bake in 350°F oven for 10 to 12 minutes, or until golden, stirring once or twice. Remove and transfer nuts to piece of foil to cool. (Pecans can be made up to several months in advance and kept in airtight container.) Makes 1 cup.

Apple-Walnut Vinaigrette

½ of tart green apple, peeled, cored, and cut up
1 shallot, peeled and cut up
3 tablespoons apple cider vinegar
1½ teaspoons sugar
⅛ teaspoon kosher salt or regular salt
⅛ teaspoon pepper
¼ cup walnut oil

Place apple, shallot, vinegar, sugar, salt, and pepper in blender container. Cover and blend until nearly smooth. With blender running, gradually add oil in thin steady stream. Makes about ¾ cup. Vinaigrette can be prepared several days ahead.

Judy's Buttery Bread Bowls

3¾ to 4¼ cups bread flour
1 package active dry yeast
1½ cups milk
2 tablespoons sugar
2 tablespoons butter or margarine
1 teaspoon salt

In large mixing bowl combine 1¾ cups flour and yeast; set aside. In medium saucepan heat and stir milk, sugar, butter, and salt just until warm (120°F to 130°F)

and butter almost melts. Add milk mix to dry mixture. Beat with electric mixe low to medium speed for 30 seconds, sc ing sides of bowl constantly. Beat on speed 3 minutes. Using wooden spoor in as much of remaining flour as possil

Turn dough out onto lightly floured face. Knead in enough remaining flo make moderately stiff dough that is sm and elastic (6 to 8 minutes total). Sl dough into ball. Place in lightly gre bowl, turning once to grease surfac dough. Cover loosely with plastic w leaving room for dough to rise. Chi refrigerator overnight.

Let dough stand at room tempera 10 minutes. Grease very large cookie sl set aside. Grease large sheet of w paper; set aside. Divide dough int pieces. Shape each piece into ball (a 2½ inches across), pulling edges unde make smooth top. Using floured scis snip 2 slits across top of each roll, forr "X." Place balls on prepared cookie sl Cover with greased waxed paper, gre side down. Let rise in warm place nearly double in size (1 to 1¼ ho Remove waxed paper.

Bake in 350°F oven about 15 minute until golden and rolls sound hollow w you tap top with your fingers. Immedia remove rolls from sheet. Cool comple on wire racks. When cool, cut about 1- slice from top of each roll; reserve t Hollow out bread leaving ½-inch s (Reserve removed bread for another u Cover bread shells and tops until ser time. Makes 6 bread bowls.

Spring Lamb Stew

¼ cup all-purpose flour
1 teaspoon salt
½ teaspoon pepper
1½ pounds lean boneless lamb should or sirloin, cut into 1-inch cubes
¼ cup extra-virgin olive oil or cooking
4 cloves garlic, minced
⅓ cup dry red wine
2½ cups chicken stock or broth
1 bay leaf
1 tablespoon snipped fresh rosemary
2 medium potatoes, cut in ¾-inch cub
2 cups sliced fresh mushrooms (such a button, crimini, shiitake, oyster, and/or chanterelle)
2 cups peeled, cubed butternut squas (one 14- to 16-ounce squash)
1 cup sliced carrots
2 medium leeks, halved and sliced (⅔ cup)
Roasted asparagus

Continued on page 186

Easy to use.

AMERICA ONLINE VERSION 6.0!

- *Easy to install and even easier to get started*
- *Parental Controls help safeguard your kids online*
- *Free 24-hour customer service means help is just a phone call away*
- *Keep in touch with friends & family with convenient, easy-to-use
  e-mail, Buddy List® and Instant Message℠ features*

Hard to resist.

CALL 1-800-4-ONLINE TODAY FOR FREE AOL 6.0 SOFTWARE AND 700 HOURS TO TRY IT OUT!

AMERICA Online®

*So easy to use,
no wonder it's #1*

Continued from page 184

In self-sealing plastic bag shake together flour, salt, and pepper. Add lamb cubes and shake to coat. In very large skillet brown lamb cubes, half at a time, in hot olive oil. Remove lamb cubes from skillet. Add garlic and cook and stir 30 seconds. Add red wine, stirring to scrape up browned bits. Return lamb cubes to skillet. Add chicken stock, bay leaf, and rosemary. Bring to boiling; reduce heat.

Cover and simmer for 30 minutes. Add cubed potatoes. Return to boiling, reduce heat, and simmer, covered, 15 minutes more. Add mushrooms, squash, and carrots and cook, covered, 10 minutes more. Add leeks and cook, covered, 10 minutes more. Remove bay leaf and discard. Serve in bread bowls placed in soup plates, with roasted asparagus on side. Makes 6 servings.

Fresh Pineapple and Dried Cherry Upside-Down Cake

2⅓ cups sifted cake flour
1 tablespoon baking powder
¼ teaspoon salt
⅓ cup unsalted butter, melted
1 cup packed dark brown sugar
8 (¼-inch-thick) slices cored and peeled
   fresh pineapple (about 15 ounces)
½ cup dried cherries
½ cup unsalted butter, softened
1¼ cups granulated sugar
2 vanilla beans, scraped, or 2 teaspoons
   vanilla
3 eggs
¾ cup whole milk
Whipped cream (optional)

Butter and flour 10x2-inch round cake pan. In medium bowl stir together flour, baking powder, and salt; set aside. Stir together ⅓ cup melted butter and brown sugar; pat mixture with your fingers into bottom of prepared pan. Arrange pineapple slices over brown sugar mixture in pan, cutting slices and overlapping as necessary. Sprinkle evenly with cherries.

In large mixing bowl, beat ½ cup butter, granulated sugar, and vanilla until combined. Add eggs, one at a time, beating after each addition until combined. Alternately add milk, ¼ cup at a time, and dry ingredients, beating until just combined. Spoon batter into prepared pan, spreading to edges.

Bake in 350°F oven about 1 hour or until toothpick inserted near center comes out clean. Cool 5 minutes in pan on wire rack. Invert onto large cake plate. Cool about 1 hour before serving. Serve warm, with whipped cream, if desired. Makes 12 servings.

Espresso Granita with Crea

1 cup water
½ cup sugar
½ vanilla bean, split
2 strips orange peel (about 3x1 inche
1 cup freshly brewed espresso
1 cup whipped cream
1 tablespoon finely shredded orange

In medium saucepan combine water, s vanilla bean, and orange peel. Bring to ing. Remove from heat; stir in espr Strain mixture through fine sieve; dis solids. Transfer liquid mixture to glass pan or shallow baking dish. Cover freeze overnight or until solid.

Scrape large spoon across surfac frozen granita, spooning dessert into cold glass espresso cups or champ glasses. Top with whipped cream and ly shredded orange peel. Serve immed ly. Makes 6 to 8 servings.

Raspberry and Cream Chee Stuffed French Toast

1 (8-ounce) package cream cheese,
   softened
12 (¾-inch-thick) slices day-old brioch
   challah, or other egg bread (abou
   one-pound loaf)
1 cup fresh raspberries*
3 eggs, beaten
¾ cup half-and-half, light cream, or m
3 tablespoons sugar
½ teaspoon vanilla
Dash salt
Pure maple syrup or maple-flavored s
   (optional)

Spread cream cheese evenly over one of each slice of bread. Top half of slic bread with raspberries. Top with remai bread slices, cream cheese side dow make "sandwiches." Combine beaten half-and-half, sugar, vanilla, and salt in low bowl. Dip each sandwich in egg ture, turning carefully to coat both s Place sandwiches in greased 15x10x1- baking pan. Bake in 425°F oven 15 mir or until golden brown, turning once 10 minutes. Serve warm with maple sy if desired. Makes 6 servings

*If desired, you can substitute frozen berries. Thaw and drain; reserve juic another use. ⌖

Queen size Rutherford Bed ($1099) shown with Charlton cotton sheets and skirt with Tribeca linen duvet and shams.

CHARLES P. ROGERS

Original 19th and 20th century brass and iron beds and traditional European bed linens are now available direct from America's premier bed maker since 1855. Call 1-800-272-7726 or visit www.charlesprogers.com to request a catalog and sale price list. Factory showroom open to the public.

NEW YORK: 55 WEST 17 STREET (5-6 AVES) NYC, 212-675-4400. OUT OF STATE 1-800-272-7726. **NEW JERSEY:** 300 RTE. 17 NORTH, EAST RUTHERFORD (CLOSED SUN), 201-933-8300.
OPEN DAILY, SATURDAY, SUNDAY. PHONE ORDERS WELCOME. WE SHIP ANYWHERE.

READER'S RESOURCI

COVER
See sources listed for "The Little Mansion,"
page 123.

PAGE 8
FROM THE EDITOR
Slipper chair (Thomas O'Brien Collection):
Hickory Chair, 800/349-4579.

PAGES 24–26
TRENDS:
OPTICAL ALLUSIONS
Pages 24–26—**Barbara Barry Collection**
(Oval X-back armchair in Java finish; oval X-
back side chair in Java finish; #3491 ottoman in
Java finish): through Baker Furniture, 800/592-
2537. **Geometri and Optik fabrics** (by
Verner Panton): Maharam, 800/645-3943, trade
only. **Checker Split, Double Triangles,**
Facets fabrics (by Alexander Girard):
Maharam, 800/645-3943, trade only.

PAGES 28–36
DECORATING:
DOWN TO THE LAST INCH
Interior designer: Beverly Flynn Ritchie,
Flynn Ritchie Interiors, 3317 Cleveland Ave.
N.W., Washington, D.C. 20008; 202/333-8627.
Pages 28–30. Living room—**Drapery** (stripe):
Jim Thompson Thai Silk, 800/262-0336, trade
only. **Drapery** (Belvoir Silk): Hinson & Co.,
212/688-5538, trade only. **Drapery trim** (GRK
Trims): The Rist Corp., 202/646-1540, trade

only. **Open armchairs, slant-top desk**:
Trouvailles Inc., 617/489-8777. **Bronze**
sculpture: Gore Dean Antiques, 202/625-1776;
www.gore-dean.com.
Pages 32–34. Dining room—**Table**, **chairs**,
small chest: owner's collection.
Page 36. Kitchen—**Cabinets** (cherry): custom.
Stools: Ballard Designs, 800/367-2775.
Refrigerator, cooktop: GE Appliances,
800/626-2000. **Countertops**: granite. Kitchen
sitting area—**Drapery** (Greenwich glazed
chintz/black #79363-970): Brunschwig & Fils,
800/538-1880, trade only. **Drapery banding**
(Johanna, discontinued): Pierre Frey, 212/213-
3099, trade only. **Undercurtain** (Tattersall
check #39168, Payne): Westgate Fabrics,
800/527-6666, trade only. **Carpet**
(Monaco/Forest sisal): Hollis & Spencer Ltd.,
212/488-0240, trade only.

PAGES 40–48
ARTISAN:
MASTER OF MINUSCULE
E.J. Kupjack Associates Inc., 12 Main St., Park
Ridge, IL 60068; 847/823-6661.

PAGES 62–68
PERSONAL ARCHITECTURE:
IT'S A SMALL WORLD
Rinfret playhouse: Amish Outdoor Living,
888/264-7487. **Sisal rug**: Ballard Designs,
800/367-2775; www.ballarddesigns.com.
Fabric: Brunschwig & Fils, 800/538-1880,
trade only.
Pennell playhouses: Little Mansions,
610/444-5754; www.little-mansions.com.

PAGES 72–80
DEFINING STYLE:
PALACE PORCELAIN
Read all about it: *Porcelain for Palaces: The*
Fashion for Japan in Europe 1650–1750, by
John Ayers, Oliver Impey, and J.V.G. Mallet,
Oriental Ceramic Society, 1990 (approximately
$70), is an excellent reference guide to early
Imari. (www.bibliofind.com).
For the later period, check out Nancy Schiffer's
Japanese Porcelain 1800–1950, Schiffer
Publishing Co., 1999 ($59.95).
Where to see it: The Peabody Essex Museum
in Salem, Massachusetts, has one of the world's
most comprehensive collections of Asian export
art, housed in its own wing. Before going, call
to find out how much Imari is on display;
978/745-9500.

PAGES 88–94
SHOWHOUSE SHOWCASE:
CLASSICS REFRESHED
Young Women's League of
New Canaan Showhouse
New Canaan, Connecticut
Interior designer: Ron Cacciola, Ron
Cacciola Interior Planners, 993 Post Rd. E.
Westport, CT 06880; 203/222-1002.
Page 88. Sitting room—**All items:** available
through Ron Cacciola Interior Planners,
203/222-1002.

Junior League of Boston Showhouse
Boston, Massachusetts
Interior designer: Wendy Reynolds, Chee
House, 14 Cheever Circle, Andover, MA 01
978/475-4931.
Page 90. Parlor—**Sofa** (O'Henry House),
tufted-back chair (O'Henry House), **love**
seat (O'Henry House), **slipcovered**
Chippendale side chair (David Salmon):
Webster & Co., 617/261-9660, trade only. **S**
fabric (chenille damask #400397), **chair fa**
(linen floral print, Carnevalet #102317), **lov**
seat fabric (linen floral print, Carnevalet
#102317), **slipcover fabric** for chair (dama
Elephant Walk #401361), **table skirt** (Kinc
#400751): Travers, 212/888-7900, trade only
George III armchair (slipcovered in flam
stitch, Excelsior #6005-10): Rose Cumming
Ltd., 212/758-0844, trade only. **Table-skirt**
fringe (Smith & Brighty): Webster & Co.,
617/261-9660, trade only. **Benches** (David
Salmon): Webster & Co., 617/261-9660, tra
only. **Table**: Mrs. MacDougall,
through Hinson & Co., 212/688-7754, trade
only. **George I-style secretary** in burled v
(TV cabinet), **Georgian-style tea table**:
William Switzer & Assoc. Ltd., 604/255-591
trade only.

Duxbury Historical Society Showhouse
Duxbury, Massachusetts
Interior designer: Kim Barrett, Clara Hay
Barrett Designs, 300 Boylston St., Boston,
02116; 617/426-6144.
Page 92. Drawing room—**Rug** (custom): St
Carpet Corp., 212/752-9000, trade only.
Furniture, accessories, drapery fabric:
Clara Hayes Barrett Designs, 617/426-6144
Toile fabric (Ballon de Gonesse/Vert 4257
104): Quadrille Wallpapers and Fabrics,
212/753-2995, trade only.

Continued on page 190

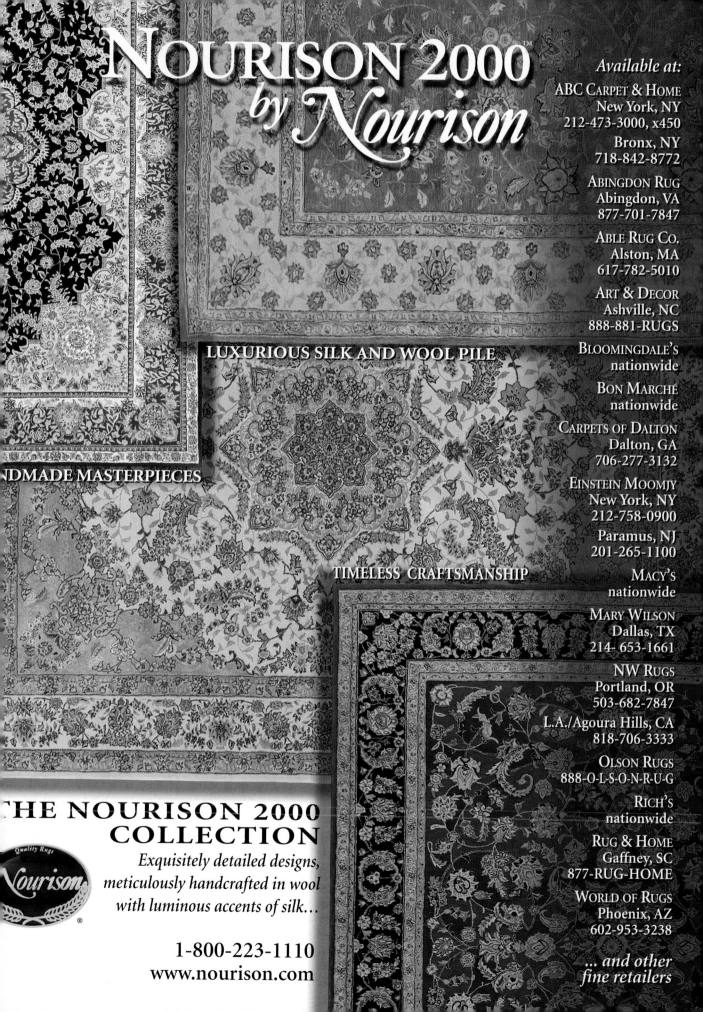

READER'S RESOURCE Continued from page 188

Pasadena Showcase House of Design
Pasadena, California

Interior designer: John Cole, John Cole Interior Design, 8866 Collingwood Dr., Los Angeles, CA 90069; 310/652-6288.

Page 94. Living room—**Compton tight-back sofa; Compton tight-back chairs:** John Cole Interior Design, 310/652-6288. **All fabrics and trims, mohair-covered armchair and settee:** Brunschwig & Fils, 800/538-1880, trade only. **Fabric for yellow sofas** (Gwendolen Lampas/Jasmine #89323-342), **trim** (Othello large cord with tape #90526/1783); **Compton sofa fabric** (Akbar woven paisley/Golden Rose #39713/01, discontinued), **trim** (Margay chenille cord on tape/ brick red #39030.181 and Margay chenille tape #39034/181); **Compton chair fabric** (Metropolitan mohair velvet/Tobacco #6313.01/11), **trim** (Margay chenille cord/Topaz #39030.335); **living room drapery and matching chair fabric** (Couronne Imperiale cotton print/Rose #65341.01), **drapery trim** (Gabrielle tassel fringe/yellow and multi #90468.05/30); **chair trim** (Gabrielle small gimp/red #90474.05/21, discontinued); **bay window drapery fabric** (Fany striped silk print/Strawberry #71262-136); **fireplace chair fabric** (Polo antiqued leather/Hazelnut #2630.00/3); **piano bench fabric** (Milano figured woven/Bronze #46053.02); **stool fabric** (Elefantes cotton print/Jade #50964.01), **trim** (Traviata fringe/Noisette/ green, rose and gold #90503.05/10); **table skirt** (Rembrandt cotton velvet/green #89333-435, discontinued), **trim** (Frange Torse fringe/Savane, 8-inch #90537/20); **tabletop fabric** (Medici plaid taffeta/seafoam, celadon, lime, and pine #60054.01), **trim** (Lionello ball fringe/coral and ivy #39044-M64); **pillow with dove** (Les Colombes silk warp print/cream #71173-015), **trim** (Sourire De Soie tassel fringe 3/mint and ecru #90605/15); **blue pillows** (Favorite Lampas/powder blue #81841-204), **trim** (Applause small cord on tape/canary, rose and green #90622/7); **blue and cream striped pillows** (Montabert taffeta stripe/blue and white #30162.00); **blue plaid taffeta pillows** (Romeo taffeta plaid/Delft #53332.01); **yellow plaid taffeta pillows** (Romeo taffeta plaid/gold #53333.01, discontinued): Brunschwig & Fils, 800/538-1880, trade only. **Carpets:** Stark Carpet Corp., 212/752-9000, trade only. **Portugese gateleg table; French stretcher table:** John Nelson Antiques, 310/652-2103. **Reproduction lamp tables; lamp tables; coffee table:** Gregorius/Pineo, 310/659-0588. **Light fixtures and lamps, blue-and-white jar, stools** (adapted by John Cole), **antique English chandelier:** Paul Ferrante Inc., 323/653-4142, trade only. **Pine cabinets** (designed by John Cole): through

Bruce Graney & Co., 626/449-9547.
Upholstered pieces (designed by John Cole): John Cole Interior Design, 310/652-6288.
Flowers (Brad Coon Custom Designs): Botanica, 323/653-8245.

PAGES 116–120
KITCHENS:
MAKING ROOM IN
A SMALL KITCHEN

Kitchen designer: Cheryl Hamilton-Gray, Hamilton-Gray Design, 5786 Jeffries Ranch Rd., Oceanside, CA 92057; 760/758-5702. Cheryl Hamilton was formerly with Chicago Kitchen & Bath.

Pages 116–118. Kitchen—**Cabinetry** (Leicht): available through Chicago Kitchen & Bath, 312/642-8844. **Dishwasher:** Miele Inc., 800/843-7231. **Tile:** Ann Sacks Tile & Stone, 800/278-8453. **Countertop** (Corian): Dupont Corian, 800/426-7426; www.corian.com. **Sink:** Franke Kitchen Systems Div., 800/626-5771. **Faucets:** Kroin Inc., 800/655-7646. **Chrome rods:** Hafele America Co., 800/334-1873. **Wall treatment:** Charlotte Faubion, through Hamilton-Gray Design, 760/758-5702. **Antique bench:** Malcolm Franklin Antiques, 312/227-0202. **Stove:** Viking Range Corp., 888/845-4641; www.vikingrange.com. **Stove hood, worktables** (designed by Cheryl Hamilton-Gray): Hamilton-Gray Design, 760/758-5702. **Stove hood fabrication:** Chicago Brass Inc., 847/926-0001; www.chicagobrass.com. **Worktable countertops** (Black Absolute Granite): Carrara Marble, 773/237-0415. **Refrigerator:** Sub-Zero Freezer Co. Inc., 800/222-7820; www.subzero.com. **Microwave:** KitchenAid, 800/422-1230. **Oven:** Gaggenau USA Corp., 800/828-9165; www.gaggenau.com. Page 120. Service bar area—**Tile:** Ann Sacks Tile & Stone, 800/278-8453. **Cabinetry** (Leicht): available through Chicago Kitchen & Bath, 312/642-8844. **Wall treatment:** Charlotte Faubion, through Hamilton-Gray Design, 760/758-5702. **Countertop** (stainless, designed by Cheryl Hamilton-Gray): Hamilton-Gray Design, 760/758-5702. **Countertop fabrication:** Chicago Brass Inc., 847/926-0001; www.chicagobrass.com.

PAGES 123–131
THE LITTLE MANSION

Interior designers: Sheila Barron, Laura Stoll, Barron & Stoll Interior Design, 2402 Lincoln St., Evanston, IL 60201; 847/864-4778. **Architect:** James Landaker, Landaker Architects, 847/945-7975. **Garden designer:** Charlotte Jones Garden Design, 847/842-8820. Pages 123–127. Living room—**Wall paint** (custom), **trim** (Linen White #70): Benjamin Moore & Co., 888/236-6667. **Fireplace** (design by Sheila Barron): Barron & Stoll Interior

Design, 847/864-4778. **Chair fabric** (ivory chenille): Betterman's Inc., 312/644-4073. **Chair fabric** (copper chenille): Pindler & Pindler Inc., 800/669-6002, trade only. **Painting** over fireplace; **candelabra:** Don Stuart Antiques, 847/501-4454. **Drapery:** Boussac Fadini Inc., 212/421-0534, trade o... **Drapery fabrication:** Dezign Sewing Inc 773/549-4336. **Pillow fabric:** Christopher Norman Inc., 212/647-0303, trade only. **Pil... fabric:** Randolph & Hein Inc., 800/844-99... trade only. **Sofa:** Eurocraft Inc., 312/850-0... **Sofa pillows** (designed by Sheila Barron): Barron & Stoll Interior Design, 847/864-47... **Club chair** (antique): Donald Stuart Antic... 847/501-4454. **Upholstery fabric** (Rando... Alexander): Betterman's Inc., 312/644-407... **Coffee table** (Barbara Barry): Baker Furniture, 800/592-2537, trade only. **End ...** (antique): Antique Resources, 773/871-424... **Crystal lamps** (Vaughan Lamps): Kirk-Brummel Associates, 212/477-8590, trade ... **Chair** at desk (antique): Donald Stuart Antiques, 847/501-4454. **Chair fabric:** Bo... Fadini Inc., 212/421-0534, trade only. **Tas...** Merwitz Textiles, 312/664-0662. Exterior—**Trim paint** (Linen White): Benjamin Moo... Co., 888/236-6667. Dining area—**Table** (antique): Donald Stuart Antiques, 847/501...4454. **Chairs:** B.J. Furniture & Antiques, 773/262-1000. **Chair fabric** (ivory chenille... Betterman's Inc., 312/644-4073. **Tassels:** Merwitz Textiles, 312/664-0662. Kitchen—**Cabinetry** (custom, mahogany chest desig... by Sheila Barron): Barron & Stoll Interior Design, 847/864-4778. **Cabinetry fabrica...** Hoffmann Custom Designs Inc., 847/362-9... **Sink:** Franke Kitchen Systems Div., 800/6... 5771. **Rug:** Job Youshaei Rug Co., 847/432... 8100. **Stove:** Viking Range Corp., 888/845-4641; www.vikingrange.com.
Pages 128–129. Powder room—**Mural:** by artist Curtis Bewley, 773/274-2263. **Sink** (Corian top and bowl): Hoffmann Custom Designs Inc., 847/362-9404. **Sconces** (anti... Lang Levin Studios Ltd., 312/644-7064. **Gi... console:** owner's collection. Loft—**Screen** (antique): Donald Stuart Antiques, 847/501...4454. **Sofa** (designed by Sheila Barron); **ch...** Eurocraft Inc., 312/850-0071. **Upholstery fabric:** Brunschwig & Fils, 800/538-1880,... only. **Pillows** (designed by Sheila Barron); **quilt** (antique): Barron & Stoll Interior De... 847/864-4778. **Chandelier** (antique); **sha...** (custom): Lang Levin Studios Ltd., 312/64... 7064. **Drapery** (designed by Sheila Barron... **ceiling** (tray ceiling, custom color, designe... Sheila Barron); **wall paint** (custom): Barro... Stoll Interior Design, 847/864-4778. **Carp...** Village Carpets, 847/446-3800.
Pages 130–131. Master bedroom—**Wall**

Continued on page 192

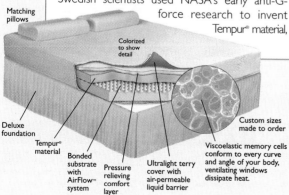

READER'S RESOURCE Continued from page 190

covering (Peterson/Piazza, linen): Decorators Walk, 516/249-3100, trade only. **Headboard** (designed by Sheila Barron), **bed linens:** fabricated by Eurocraft Inc., 312/850-0071. **Rug:** Village Carpets, 847/446-3800. **Lamps:** Mrs. MacDougall at Hinson Lighting Inc., 212/688-7754, trade only. **Upholstery fabric** (linen): Decorators Walk, 516/249-3100, trade only. **Bureau** (antique), **painting** (antique): Donald Stuart Antiques, 847/501-4454. Master bathroom—**Sconces:** Kirk-Brummel Associates, 212/477-8590, trade only. **Sink** (Corian): Hoffmann Custom Designs Inc., 847/362-9404. **Cabinet** (designed by Sheila Barron): Barron & Stoll Interior Design, 847/864-4778. **Mirror** (antique); **stool** (antique): owner's collection.

PAGES 132–141
A GEM OF A GARDEN

Architect: Richard L. Olsen, G.O. Design, 632 N. Lincoln St., Hinsdale, IL 60521; 630/887-1405. **Garden designer:** Craig Bergmann, Craig Bergmann Landscape Design, 1924 Lake Ave., Wilmette, IL 60091; 847/251-8355. **Contractor:** Kenna Co., 325 Ridge Ave., Clarendon Hills, IL 60514; 630/986-9067. **Nursery:** Craig Bergmann's Country Garden, 700 Kenosha Rd., Winthrop Harbor, IL 60096-0424; 847/746-0311. **Nursery:** The Growing Place Nursery & Flower Farm Inc., 25 W. 471 Plank Rd., Naperville, IL; 630/355-4000. **Nursery:** Vern Goers Greenhouse, 5620 S. Oak St., Hinsdale, IL 60521; 630/323-1085. **Nursery:** The Hidden Gardens, 16 W. Frontage Rd., Hinsdale, IL 60521; 630/655-8283.
Pages 132–133. Exterior—**Painting:** Peter Zaagman Inc., 630/789-2942. **Antique bricks:** Colonial Brick Co., 312/733-2600. **Frog:** owner's collection. Entrance—**Benches:** Architectural Artifacts Inc., 773/348-0622. **Cushions and awnings:** Williams Awning Co., 800/227-6606. **Antique butler:** The Courtyard (consignment shop), 630/323-1135. **Baskets on gates:** Kane County Flea Market, 630/377-2252. Pages 134–137. Patio—**White chairs:** L.L. Bean Inc., 800/809-7057. **Brick and stonework:** Salvador Guzman Landscaping, 630/655-4236. **Table, small fence:** The Cottage Collection, 708/246-8568. **Birdhouses:** owner's collection. Pond and bench—**Bench:** owner's collection. **Pond:** Salvador Guzman Landscaping, 630/655-4236. Birdbath—**Birdbath:** Craig Bergmann's Country Garden, 847/746-0311. **Benches:** Architectural Artifacts

Inc., 773/348-0622. **Cushions:** Williams Awning Co., 800/227-6606.
Pages 138–139. Arbor—**Arbor:** Kenna Co., 630/986-9067. **Table** (custom): owner's collection. **Chairs:** Smith & Hawken, 800/776-3336. **Wire basket chandelier:** Lexington Gardens, 212/861-4390. **Three-tier planter:** Treillage, 212/535-2288. **Stones:** Craig Bergmann's Country Garden, 847/746-0311. Garage and gate—**Horse head** on garage: Antiques on Old Plank Rd., 630/971-0500. **Lavabo** on gate (antique): owner's collection. Pages 140–141. Cutting garden—**Trellis, potting table:** owner's collection.

PAGES 142–153
BEAUTY BY THE BEACH

Interior designer: Cher Beall, Cashmere and Co., 5 Civic Plaza, Suite 320, Newport Beach, CA 92660; 949/718-6340.
Pages 142–147. Living room—**Sofa:** Moyes Custom Furniture, 714/630-8210. **Slipcover on club chair, sofa:** Classy Scraps, 714/957-3388. **Slipcover fabric** (Home Couture, 323/936-1302, trade only): available through Thomas Lavin Showroom, 310/278-2456. **Ottoman** (Aston Garrett): through Cashmere and Co., 949/718-6340. **Ottoman fabric:** Robert Allen, 800/240-8189, trade only. **Piano** (Boston): Field's Piano, 714/662-2117. **Piano bench:** Charles Pollock Reproductions, 323/653-5794, trade only. **Bench upholstery:** Universal Upholstery, 949/494-6403. **Italian chair:** Hamilton Inc., 323/655-9193. **Chair fabric** (Home Couture, 323/936-1302, trade only): available through Thomas Lavin Showroom, 310/278-2456. **Lamp** on piano: La Bella Copia-Bella Shades, 415/255-0452. **Lampshade:** Palmer Design, 858/576-1350, trade only. **Large lamps:** Panache, 323/441-9600. **End table:** Hamilton Inc., 323/655-9193. **Framing:** Scene Gallery, 949/720-3939. **Framing:** Jefferies Ltd., 949/642-4154. **Drapery:** Stevens Custom Drapery, 714/996-6092. **Drapery fabric** (linen): Kravet, 800/648-4686. **Fauteuil:** Minton-Spidell Inc., 310/657-0160, trade only. **Fabric** (Home Couture, 323/936-1302, trade only): available through Thomas Lavin Showroom, 310/278-2456; and Summer Hill Ltd., 650/363-2600, trade only. **Antique prints:** Devine Antique Print Gallery, 626/793-8073. **Rug** (leather-bound sea grass): Creative Flooring Resources, 512/478-3010. **Floor lamps:** Palmer Design, 858/576-1350, trade only. **Candlesticks:** Lee Stanton Antiques, 949/240-5181. **Desk:** Dennis &

Lean, 310/652-0855, trade only. **Table:** Sto Yard Inc., 858/586-1580, trade only. **Table lamps:** Nancy Corzine, 310/559-9051. **Din chair fabric:** Robert Allen, 800/240-8189, trade only.
Pages 148–149. Kitchen—**Table:** Quacken & Winkler, 310/657-3400, trade only. **Chai** Lockhart Furniture, 562/941-5822. **Chair fabric:** Summer Hill Ltd., 650/363-2600, tr only. **Slipcover fabrication:** Classy Scraps 714/957-3388. **Framing:** Jefferies Ltd., 949/642-4154. **Painted chest:** Carter Brow 949/645-3730. **Armchair slipcover:** Classy Scraps, 714/957-3388. **Armchair fabric** (Home Couture, 323/936-1302, trade only) available through Thomas Lavin Showroom 310/278-2456. **French chair:** Charles Poll Reproductions, 323/653-5794, trade only. **Chair fabric:** Brunschwig & Fils, 800/538-1880, trade only. **Lamps:** Lee Stanton Antiques, 949/240-5181. **Wall faux finish:** Delmar Studio, 323/938-5826. **Backsplash tile:** Concept Studio, 949/759-0606, trade Family room—**Bergère:** Charles Pollock Reproductions, 323/653-5794, trade only. **Fabric:** Brunschwig & Fils, 800/538-1880, trade only. **Side chair:** Minton-Spidell Inc. 310/657-0160, trade only. **Fabric:** Brunsch & Fils, 800/538-1880, trade only, and Summ Hill Ltd., 650/363-2600, trade only. **Fruit basket lamp:** Charles Pollock Reproductio 323/653-5794, trade only. **Round French table:** Adel Kerr Furnishings, 214/741-485 trade only. **Sofa:** Moyes Custom Furniture 714/630-8210. **Lamp:** Lee Stanton Antique 949/240-5181. **Drapery:** Tabors, 915/942-1 **Fabric:** Brunschwig & Fils, 800/538-1880, trade only. **Rug** (sea grass): Creative Floor Resources, 512/478-3010.
Pages 150–151. Master bedroom—**Bed** (custom): Universal Upholstery, 949/494-64 **Desk:** Niermann Weeks, 212/319-7979, tra only. **Framing:** Nelson Picture Framing, 949/494-6696. **Chairs:** Rose Tarlow-Melro House, 323/651-2202, trade only. **Fabric:** Schumacher, 800/988-7775, trade only. **La** Palmer Design, 858/576-1350, trade only. **Shades:** Carol's Roman Shades, 805/489-4 Dressing area—**Chest:** Niermann Weeks, 212/319-7979, trade only. **Ottoman** (custo Universal Upholstery, 949/494-6403. **Wallpaper:** Osborne & Little, 212/751-33 trade only. **Drapery:** Tabors, 915/942-169(**Fabric:** Kravet, 800/648-4686. **Antique lamps:** Lee Stanton Antiques, 949/240-518

Continued on page 194

Traditional Home® (ISSN-0883-4660) is published bimonthly in March, May, July, September, November, and December at $22 a year by the Magazine Group of Meredith Corporation, 1716 St., Des Moines, IA 50309-3023. Periodicals postage paid at Des Moines, Iowa, and at additional mailing offices. Canada Post Publications Mail Sales Product Agreement No. 1369342. Canac 12348 2887 RT. Canadian Return Address: TRADITIONAL HOME, 2744 EDNA STREET, WINDSOR, ONTARIO N8Y 1V2. © Copyright Meredith Corporation 2001. All rights reserved. Printed in SUBSCRIPTION PRICES: one year, $22 in the United States and its possessions; Canada and other countries add $8 per year. POSTMASTER: Send address changes to Traditional Home, P. 37275, Boone, IA 50037-0275.

THE SIXTH ANNUAL TRADITIONAL HOME SHOWHOUSE TOUR

PRESENTED BY

 **ce Pfister**™   **GMC.**   **KitchenAid®**
FOR THE WAY IT'S MADE.®

WE ARE PROFESSIONAL GRADE.™

SPRING 2001

March 29–April 14 **2001 American Red Cross Designers' Show House @ City Place**
West Palm Beach, FL
(561) 833-7711

April 21–May 6 **Junior League of Nashville's Decorators' Show House 2001**
Nashville, TN
(615) 269-9393 x110

April 21–May 13 **Atlanta Symphony Associates Decorators' Showhouse**
Atlanta, GA
(404) 733.4935

April 24–May 20 **Kips Bay Boys & Girls Club Decorator Show House**
New York, NY
(718) 893-8600

April 28–May 20 **The Lake Forest Showcase House & Gardens**
Lake Forest, IL
(847) 604-3479

May 1–May 25 **Junior League of Boston Decorators' Showhouse**
Boston, MA
(617) 422-1907

May 5–May 28 **Vassar Showhouse/The Woods**
Philidelphia, PA
(610) 527-9717

FALL 2001

October **National Symphony Orchestra Decorators' Show House**
Washington, DC
(202) 416-8150

October **2001 Symphony Guild ASID Showhouse**
Charlotte, NC
(704) 525-0522

For *Traditional Home* subscription information, please call 1-800-374-8791.
For *Decorator Showhouse*, please call 1-800-556-9184. Visit *Traditional Home* on
the worldwide web at www.designerfinder.com.

Traditional Home is proud to announce its 2001 Showhouse Tour members! Now entering its sixth year, this national program continues to be the only one of its kind. Each year *Traditional Home* visits the country's most prestigious showhouses featuring the design and decorative masterpieces of today's top interior designers. What's more, all tour proceeds support local charities.

Traditional Home, the magazine dedicated to bringing you new, yet classic design ideas, and *Decorator Showhouse*, the only magazine devoted exclusively to the world of showhouses, hope you will join us at a showhouse near you!

Reader's Resource Continued from page 192
Rug (sea grass): Creative Flooring Resources, 512/478-3010.
Pages 152–153. Boy's bedroom—**Rug:** ABC Carpet & Home, 212/473-3000. **Child's table:** Thea Segal Design, 818/765-8115. **Bed** (leathe Universal Upholstery, 949/494-6403. **Wall pap** Ralph Lauren Home, 800/578-7656. **Stool:** Pla Jane Inc., 212/595-6916. Boy's bathroom— **Hanging rug:** Claire Murray, 800/252-4733. **Chair fabric:** Schumacher, 800/988-7775, trac only. **Pillow fabric:** Bergamo Fabrics Inc., 212/462-1010, trade only. **Shower curtain:** Westgate Fabrics Inc., 800/527-6666, trade on Girl's bedroom—**Shades** (custom): Custom H Lighting, 949/642-4546. **Floral fabric:** Ralph Lauren Home: 800/578-7656. **Framing:** Art Masters, 512/491-9233. **Rug:** Masland Carpets Inc., 800/633-0468.

PAGES 154–163
MICHIGAN'S BRIGADOON
Martin residence. **Interior designer:** Elizabe Martin Interior Design, 9404 Whim Trail, Richland, MI 49083; 616/629-5515. **Contract** Mike McMinn, 9167 Guernsey Lake Rd., Delt MI 49046; 616/623-5714.
Pages 154–155. Exterior—**Awnings:** Roots Ca 616/685-5063.
Pages 156, 157–158. Living room fireplace are **Carpet:** Masland Carpets Inc., 800/633-0468. **Mantel** (custom): Mike McMinn, 616/623-571 **Rocking chair, vintage table, stone firepla French doors:** owner's collection. Living/dinir room—**Carpet:** Masland Carpets Inc., 800/63 0468. **Sofas and fabric:** Lee Industries, 800/8 7150; www.leeindustries.com. **Coffee table, painted chest, dining table:** Lexington Furniture Industries, 336/249-5300. **Rug:** The Market, 800/422-4354. **Sailboat chandelier:** Welling Ripley & Labs, 616/375-5900. **Wicker settee, dining chairs, shelf:** owner's collectio

DeNooyer residence. **Contractor:** Mike McM 9167 Guernsey Lake Rd., Delton, MI 49046; 616/623-5714. **Builders:** Pete Karson, Kevan The Renaissance Builders, 616/349-8888.
Page 156–157. Exterior—**Adirondack chairs:** Doug Knibbe, Knibbe's Custom Wood Shop, 616/343-6790. **Awnings:** Roots Canvas, 616/68 5063. Living room—**Flowered cushion fabri** Brunschwig & Fils, 800/538-1880, trade only. The Rug Market, 800/422-4354. **Tea table:** Kalamazoo Antiques Market, 616/226-9788. **Piano, vintage table lamp, rattan sofa, gre and pink side table:** owner's collection.
Page 163. Kitchen—**Sink, faucet:** Kohler Co. 800/456-4537; www.kohlerco.com. **Sofa and fabric:** Ditmar's Furniture Co. Inc., 616/241-3 **Dining chairs:** Attic Trash & Treasures, 616/ 2189. **Wooden blinds:** Pier 1 Imports, 800/44 4371; www.pier1.com. **Paint** (custom): Benjam Moore & Co., 888/236-6667; www.benjaminmoore.com. Sleeping porch— **Comforter:** Ralph Lauren Home, 800/578-76

, bed skirt: Laura Ashley, 800/367-2000.

...n residence. **Interior designer:** Susan
...n Interiors, 4030 Bronson Blvd., Kalamazoo,
...9008; 616/381-1845.

...157. Porch—**Wicker furniture:**
.../Flanders Industries Inc., 888/227-8252.
...en cushion fabric: Denning Upholstery,
...882-2636. **Striped fabric:** Donghia
...iture/Textiles Ltd., 800/366-4442, trade only.
...r cloth: Jane Gulliver, 616/ 373-4036. **Table**
...: Lesterhouse Antiques, 616/668-3229.

...160. Living room—**Paintings:** Katie
...hardt Wellington, 908/273-9471. **Fabric** for
...hair with yellow piping: Brunschwig & Fils,
...538-1880, trade only. **Sofa fabric:** Westgate
...ics Inc., 800/527-6666;
....westgatefabrics.com. **Chair slipcover fabric:**
...eim & Romann Inc., 718/706-7000. **Drapery**
...ic: Waverly, 800/423-5881;
....decoratewaverly.com. **Chandelier:** Wm.
...rhouse Antiques, 616/668-3229. **Coffee**
...: Susan Brown Interiors, 616/381-1845.
...e rug: Stanton Carpet Corp., 800/452-4474.
...e lamps: Frederick Cooper Lamps, 773/384-
.... **Patterned rug, picnic table, quilt** on
...: owner's collection.

...162–163. Kitchen—**Sink** (stainless): Kohler
...800/456-4537; www.kohlerco.com. **Window**
...ment (Ramm, Son & Crocker): Robert Allen,
...240-8189, trade only.

...lin-Reisman residence. **Interior designer:**
...een Lewis, Concepts II Inc., 9265 Counselor's
... Suite 117, Indianapolis, IN 46240; 317/848-
.... **Contractor:** Mike McMinn, 9167 Guernsey
... Rd., Delton, MI 49046; 616/623-5714.
...ders: Pete Karson, Kevan Fisk, The
...ssance Builders, 616/349-8888.
... 164–165. Screened porch—**Wicker chairs**
...ottoman, wicker tray table: Pier 1
...rts, 800/447-4371; www.pier1.com.
...ion fabric: Sunbrella, Glen Raven Mills Inc.,
...'88-4413. **Bench:** Old Hickory Furniture Co.,
...32-2275. **Rug:** Joseph's Oriental Rug Imports,
...55-4230. **Ceramic side table, pecan table:**
...r's collection.

PAGES 164–167
CHECK MATE

...Thompson Thai Silk, 1694 Chantilly Dr.,
...ta, GA 30324; 800/262-0336, to the trade.
... 164–165. **Slipper-chair fabric**
...ng/Flambeau #3054/13); **pillow fabric**
...kla/Heliconia #3047/16); **background**
...c (Singburi/Magenta #3046/06): Jim
...npson Thai Silk, 800/262-0336,
...only. **Upholstery:** Gary Buxbaum,
...udson St., New York, NY 10013;
...41-3899. **Cappellini Stripe One rug,**
...ristine Vanderhurd, available from
...rnAge, 102 Wooster St., New York, NY
...2; 212/966-0669.
... 166–167. **Lampshade fabric** on bust

ued on page 198

INFOLINK

The source for product information from Traditional Home's top advertisers.

You can get useful ideas and product information by mail. Use the coupon in this section to order your choice of literature listed below. Each company mails the catalogs or information directly to you.

BUILDING OR REMODELING

1 **CALIFORNIA CLOSETS** — When you organize your home you simplify your life. We have solutions to help you stay organized in room after room of your home. Give yourself more room for the things that matter most in your life. CALIFORNIA CLOSETS. Free. Circle No. 1.

2 **FOUR SEASONS SUNROOMS & CONSERVATORIES** — Sunrooms, English-style conservatories, patio rooms, enclosures and skylights. MC² glass keeps out summer heat and insulates in winter. Do-it-yourself kits or full installation from our Nationwide Dealer Network. Free 48-page catalog. FOUR SEASONS SUNROOMS. Free. Circle No. 2.

3 **WOOD BEAUTIFUL®** — Minwax® Wood Beautiful, this inspirational magazine contains 36 pages filled with exciting home improvement projects, decorating ideas and expert wood finishing tips and techniques. THE THOMPSON-MINWAX COMPANY. Free. Circle No. 3.

4 **SHUTTERCRAFT** — Pictures and price lists of 5 styles of authentic pine and cedar shutters, exterior and interior, including plantation shutters with 21/2 inch louvers. We also finish paint the shutters using any national brand you specify and your selected color or mix. SHUTTERCRAFT. $1.00. Circle No. 4.

5 **TIMBERLANE WOODCRAFTERS** — Manufacturer of custom exterior wood shutters. Free 64-page color catalog available. TIMBERLANE WOODCRAFTERS. Free. Circle No. 5.

6 **WALKER ZANGER** — Bring your individual style to life with Walker Zanger's luxurious collection of Handmade Ceramic Tile, Terra Cotta and Glass. 110-page Ceramic Tile catalog. WALKER ZANGER. $16.00. Circle No. 6.

7 **WALKER ZANGER** — Express your personal vision with Walker Zanger's luxurious collection of Stone Tile, Stone Slabs and Mosaics. 110-page Stone catalog. WALKER ZANGER. $16.00. Circle No. 7.

8 **WALKER ZANGER** — Create your own unique vision in tile & stone with Walker Zanger's luxurious collection of Handmade Ceramic Tile, Terra Cotta, Stone Tile & Slabs, Mosaics and Glass. Introductory 20-page brochure. WALKER ZANGER. $2.00. Circle No. 8.

DECORATING

9 **BALLARD DESIGNS** — The catalog of style and inspiration. The exclusive furnishings, decorator accents, rugs, lighting, and art work that let you design rooms that express your point-of-view. Free catalog (U.S. requests only). BALLARD DESIGNS. Free. Circle No. 9.

10 **DRESSLER STENCIL COMPANY, INC.** — Create unique and beautiful surroundings with Jan Dressler's stencils. Over 600 unique design elements are available in our new color catalog. We also carry many accessories & how-to videos. DRESSLER STENCIL COMPANY, INC. $7.00. Circle No. 10.

11 **HEIRLOOM EUROPEAN TAPESTRIES** — 700 wall hanging classics for that perfect design, color, size & price! From France, Belgium & Italy. FREE ROD included. Art Book Catalogue (fully refundable). 325 designs/700 sizes. HEIRLOOM EUROPEAN TAPESTRIES. $30.00. Circle No. 11.

12 **LARSON-JUHL** — A great frame touches the entire room, adding elegance and personal style. For the best in custom frames, ask your custom framer for the Craig Ponzio Signature Collection by Larson-Juhl. LARSON-JUHL. Free. Circle No. 12.

13 **SLIPCOVERS BY MAIL** — Sure Fit slipcovers allow you to fall in love with your furniture again. Three sizes (chair, loveseat, sofa) fit most upholstered furniture. Stylish, machine-washable fabrics like velvet, chenille, and damask. Pillows, recliner, dining chair and wing chair covers available. SURE FIT, INC. Free. Circle No. 13.

14 **YVES DELORME** — From lush, romantic floral prints to tone-on-tone textural designs, Yves Delorme linens for bed, bath, and table offer the ultimate in personal expression. Fashionable, classic designs created by leading European designers and exquisitely crafted from natural fibers. YVES DELORME. Free. Circle No. 14.

WINDOWS AND DOORS

15 **AMERICAN BLIND AND WALLPAPER FACTORY** — Save up to 82% off national brand blinds, wallpaper & carpet. Plus free UPS shipping! Free decorating samples! Free blind sample kit and measuring guide! Free wallpaper catalog with over 700 patterns from traditional to contemporary! Free carpet brochure, your guide to carpet savings. AMERICAN BLIND AND WALLPAPER FACTORY. Free. Circle No. 15.

16 **ANDERSEN WINDOW & PATIO DOOR LIBRARY** — Building or remodeling? Get Smartcards™ and informative guides from the Andersen Literature Library. ANDERSEN WINDOWS, INC. Free. Circle No. 16.

17 **"THINK OF THE POSSIBILITIES"** — Marvin offers a 30-page catalog featuring their wood and clad wood windows and doors. Beautiful color photographs and information on Marvin's standard and custom products. MARVIN WINDOWS & DOORS. Free. Circle No. 17.

18 **PELLA WINDOWS AND DOORS** — Receive a FREE Dreambook from Pella® Windows & Doors, the company that never compromises on materials, craftsmanship, design or performance. PELLA CORPORATION. Free. Circle No. 18.

WALLS AND FLOORS

19 **AMTICO INTERNATIONAL** — Amtico resilient flooring replicates natural materials perfectly and maintains a long-lasting aesthetic appeal. Every floor is individually laid—piece by piece—to create a surface that is a delight to live with. Amtico—Every One is an Individual. Brochure. AMTICO INTERNATIONAL. Free. Circle No. 19.

20 **BRUCE HARDWOOD FLOORS** — No other floor covering adds warmth and beauty like Bruce. Select from over 300 different styles and colors, in our full-color 32-page catalog. BRUCE HARDWOOD FLOORS. Free. Circle No. 20.

21 **CARLISLE RESTORATION LUMBER** — Crafters of traditional wide plank flooring for over 35 years, in a variety of pines and hardwoods. Our 40-page full-color portfolio is available in a 12" x 12" coffee table format for your enjoyment. CARLISLE RESTORATION LUMBER. Free. Circle No. 21.

22 **CARPET EXPRESS** — For carpet, vinyl, and hardwood flooring at TRUE wholesale prices: Carpet Express, located in Dalton, GA. Brochure. CARPET EXPRESS. Free. Circle No. 22.

23 **CARPET ONE** — With the buying power of over 1300 stores, Carpet One offers a huge selection of name brand flooring, including our exclusive LEES Home Collection. Our 112-page "FlooringStyle" magazine features designer tips and trends, a vast selection of area rugs, and information on today's most popular flooring products. CARPET ONE. Free. Circle No. 23.

24 **THE HOOVER COMPANY** — Visit the Hoover website for complete information on all your floorcare needs. THE HOOVER COMPANY. Free. Circle No. 24.

25 **KARASTAN** — A classic? It's timeless styling, elegance and sophistication all woven together. It's Karastan Carpets & Rugs. KARASTAN. $3.00. Circle No. 25.

26 **MANNINGTON FLOORS** — Mannington presents fresh ideas throughout the home with vinyl, laminate and wood flooring. Only at fine flooring retailers. Design brochure. MANNINGTON. Free. Circle No. 26.

27 **MOHAWK CARPETS** — Send for free Mohawk product literature. MOHAWK INDUSTRIES, INC. Free. Circle No. 27.

28 **NOURISON RUG CORPORATION** — Creates the most exquisite carpets to fit virtually any budget or decór. NOURISON RUG CORPORATION. Free. Circle No. 28.

29 **PRATT AND LARSON CERAMICS** — Pratt & Larson offers a flexible collection of textures and patterns from classical to contemporary to arts & crafts. Design with hundreds of choices in tile and color combinations. PRATT AND LARSON CERAMICS. Free. Circle No. 29.

30 **SMITH & NOBLE RUG STUDIO** — Custom rugs! Your size, shape and design in just days. Hundreds of materials and borders. 20% – 70% off store prices. Catalog. SMITH & NOBLE RUG STUDIO. Free. Circle No. 30.

31 **STANTON CARPET** — Renowned for providing sophisticated style featuring Wilton patterns and sisals to printed carpet and unique area rugs. Brochure. STANTON CARPET CORP. Free. Circle No. 31.

32 **THIBAUT WALLCOVERINGS** — Since 1886 presents Centuries Vol. II, a collection of traditional designs with a whimsical and Asian influence. THIBAUT WALLCOVERINGS. $2.00. Circle No. 32.

33 **TUFENKIAN** — Our exquisite 200-page Full Line Catalog presents our Tibetan rugs individually, immersing you in Tufenkian's creative artistry. TUFENKIAN TIBETAN CARPETS. $20.00. Circle No. 33.

COLLECTIBLES

34 **ARTHUR'S** — A Celebration of the American Spiri A 92-page sale catalog featuring the finest in hom Decor—Baldwin, Howard Miller, Colonia Williamsburg reproductions, Madison Square, Kirk-Stieff an much, much more. ARTHUR'S. $8.00. Circle No. 34.

35 **HOBBY BUILDERS** — World's leading dollhous and miniatures catalog. Pay less for dollhouse ki and for accessories to furnish every room. HOBB BUILDERS SUPPLY. Free. Circle No. 35.

FURNITURE & ACCESSORIES

36 **ALEXANDER JULIAN AT HOME** — "Make th weekend jealous... celebrate everyday. That's m motto. Why not start at home creating a new loo with my latest furniture. It's casual. It's comfortable. Perfec for celebrating." FREE Literature. UNIVERSAL FURNITUR LIMITED. Free. Circle No. 36.

37 **LIGHTING YOUR LIFE** — Enhance the beauty o your home and create the mood of your choic with the many helpful tips presented in the beaut ful, four-color brochure. It has 27 pages overflowing with tip that tell plainly and concisely how lighting can make a bi difference in any room setting. AMERICAN LIGHTIN ASSOCIATION. $2.00. Circle No. 37.

38 **ARTE DE MEXICO** — Our lighting collection fea tures over 325 different hand-forged wrought iro lighting fixtures, available in 20 distinct hand applied finishes. ARTE DE MEXICO. $10.00. Circle No. 38.

39 **BAKER FURNITURE** — From elegant traditional t striking contemporary, Baker creates furniture c distinctive design, materials and craftsmanship fc those who appreciate the finest. BAKER FURNITURE. Fre Circle No. 39.

40 **BERNHARDT** — Furniture makers since 188 offers a variety of catalogs for living room, dinin room and bedroom. Catalog. BERNHARDT FURN TURE COMPANY. $12.00. Circle No. 40.

41 **BROYHILL** — "Visions", a beautiful 24-page full-colc decorating workbook from Broyhill offers an overvie of decorating basics that can help you create a bea tiful home environment. "Every thirty seconds, someone buy Broyhill." BROYHILL FURNITURE. $1.00. Circle No. 41.

42 **CENTURY FURNITURE** — A complete desig resource. Send for a 36-page booklet featurin bedroom, living room and dining room selectior from more than 20 of our collections. CENTURY FURNITUR INDUSTRIES. $5.00. Circle No. 42.

43 **CHARLES P. ROGERS BRASS & IRON BEDS, ES 1855** — Original 19th and 20th century heac boards, beds, canopy beds and daybeds dire from America's oldest maker of brass and iron beds. Fre color catalog and sale price list. Phone orders welcom Shipping available worldwide. CHARLES P. ROGERS BED Free. Circle No. 43.

44 **CHERRY HILL FURNITURE** — Beautiful furnitur wood pieces and upholstery. Save up to 50 everyday. In-home delivery since 1933. CHERR HILL FURNITURE & INTERIORS. Free. Circle No. 44.

45 **CLASSIC LEATHER, INC.** — Craftsmen of fine leathe furnishings for over 30 years. Classic Leather offers variety of styles and finishes to suit any lifestyl Brochure. CLASSIC LEATHER, INC. Free. Circle No. 45.

46 **CLAYTON MARCUS** — A distinctive collection fine furniture offering the style, elegance, & craft manship you can appreciate for a lifetime. Fror traditional to transitional & contemporary, Clayton Marcus the perfect compliment to any décor. Brochure. CLAYTO MARCUS. Free. Circle No. 46.

47 **CRYSTAL CHANDELIERS** — The international famous designer, James R. Moder, has just intro duced his new "Jewelry Collection" of chandelier sconces and baskets! Exquisite designs of quality importe crystal bring that special brilliance to your home and all affordable prices from $199 – $3,999. Free catalog. JAMES MODER® CRYSTAL CHANDELIER INC. Free. Circle No. 47.

48 **DREXEL HERITAGE FURNISHINGS** — Experienc furniture by Drexel Heritage. A variety of styles to world of individuals. DREXEL HERITAGE FURNISH INGS, INC. Free. Circle No. 48.

49 **THE FEDERALIST** — Specializes in handmad reproductions of original 18th and 19th centur period items. Each is made as closely as possible t the way the original was made. The catalog includes a wid range of furniture, lighting and decorative accessories. FRE in the U.S. THE FEDERALIST. Free. Circle No. 49.

50 **FRAN'S WICKER & RATTAN FURNITURE** - America's oldest and largest wicker & ratta importer. Widest selection, highest quality an guaranteed lowest prices. 2–3 weeks shipment most item New 64-page color catalog (price credited on order). FRAN WICKER & RATTAN FURNITURE. $2.00. Circle No. 50.

To Order By Phone Call Toll-Free M–F: 7 a.m. to 11 p.m. Saturday: 8 a.m. to 4:30 p.m. Central Standard Time: **1-800-547-0600**

• Please have item numbers ready • Credit Card purchases only

51 **FURNITURE DESIGN IMPORTS** — Plan a visit to our unique showroom. Authorized dealer for over 200 lines of furniture and imports. Competitive prices. Free brochure. FURNITURE DESIGN IMPORTS. Free. Circle No. 51.

52 **HABERSHAM** — Call or send for a copy of our full-color brochure showcasing many of our top-selling pieces. HABERSHAM FURNITURE. Free. Circle No. 52.

53 **HENREDON REGISTRY** — The immensely rich and varied tradition of country... in solid cherry, solid oak, solid mahogany, solid black walnut and reclaimed solid pine. Bedroom, dining room, occasional and upholstery. HENREDON FURNITURE INDUSTRIES, INC. $10.00. Circle No. 53.

54 **HICKORY CHAIR** — Presents a collection of fine wood furniture including reproductions and adaptations from famous American homes. Catalogue. HICKORY CHAIR COMPANY. $25.00. Circle No. 54.

55 **HICKORY CHAIR** — Presents a collection of fine upholstered furniture for today's lifestyles. Catalogue. HICKORY CHAIR COMPANY. $25.00. Circle No. 55.

56 **HOMECREST** — Fine casual and outdoor furniture. With a focus on comfort, quality and style, Homecrest can help you decorate your casual outdoor and indoor living areas. Send for a brochure. HOMECREST. Free. Circle No. 56.

57 **HOMELIFE FURNITURE** — HomeLife Furniture's 130 stores offer style at great prices for every room in your home. HOMELIFE FURNITURE. Free. Circle No. 57.

58 **HUNTER FAN** — Hunter offers over 100 styles of high-performance, energy-saving ceiling fans to fit any decor—all are "Quiet for Life." HUNTER FAN COMPANY. Free. Circle No. 58.

59 **HUNTINGTON HOUSE** — A distinctive collection of fine furniture which reflects the timeless sense of style and tradition you will appreciate for a lifetime. HUNTINGTON HOUSE. Free. Circle No. 59.

60 **KING HICKORY FURNITURE** — King Hickory Furniture creates the crowning touch that will add lasting elegance and comfort to every room in your home. KING HICKORY FURNITURE. Free. Circle No. 60.

61 **KING'S CHANDELIER** — Buy direct from King's, designers and manufacturers of beautiful all-crystal chandeliers, sconces and candelabra and Victorian gas reproductions. KING'S CHANDELIER CO. $5.00. Circle No. 61.

62 **LANDS' END®** — Coming Home with Lands' End®. From Supima® cotton towels and bedding to furniture and accessories for every room. Send for your free catalog. LANDS' END. Free. Circle No. 62.

63 **LANE FURNITURE** — Casual, relaxed and comfortable reflect the new Williamsburg Collection by Lane. Send $3 for a 32-page Williamsburg catalog featuring bedrooms, dining rooms, living rooms, accents and cedar chests. THE LANE CO. $3.00. Circle No. 63.

64 **LEXINGTON FURNITURE INDUSTRIES** — Quality, value, and style are yours in every Lexington collection from formal to casual, traditional to contemporary. Impressive selection of: bedroom, dining, occasional, home entertainment/office, youth, upholstery, and wicker furnishings. Brochure. LEXINGTON FURNITURE. Free. Circle No. 64.

65 **SCHONBEK CRYSTAL CHANDELIERS** — Founded in Bohemia in 1870, Schonbek is today the largest and most prestigious manufacturer of crystal chandeliers in North America. Designs include contemporary, traditional, retro and custom. Video and literature. SCHONBEK. Free. Circle No. 65.

66 **SCOTCHGARD™** — There's protection. Then there's Scotchgard™ protection. Send for more information. SCOTCHGARD. Free. Circle No. 66.

67 **SEALY** — Get the deep sleep you need with Sealy Posturepedic Crown Jewel. We support you night and day. SEALY, INC. Free. Circle No. 67.

68 **SUTER'S HANDCRAFTED FURNITURE** — Handcrafted furnishings in solid cherry, mahogany, and walnut. Suter's creates each piece in your choice of wood, hardware, and style. Color catalog. SUTER'S HANDCRAFTED FURNITURE. $5.00. Circle No. 68.

69 **THOMASVILLE** — Whatever your personal style, eclectic, traditional or casual, Thomasville's got exactly what you need to make yourself at home. Send for a free copy of our Thomasville Magazine. THOMASVILLE. Free. Circle No. 69.

70 **VANGUARD FURNITURE** — Dedicated to hand-crafted quality since 1968. Extensive line of eight-way hand-tied, uniquely crafted furniture featuring both fabric and leather upholstery, exposed wood chairs, bed room, dining and accent occasional. Brochures. VANGUARD FURNITURE. Free. Circle No. 70.

71 **WELLINGTON'S FURNITURE** — Leather furniture direct from North Carolina. Take this opportunity to shop our complete leather catalog. Representing only today's top American manufacturers. Styles from traditional to contemporary. WELLINGTON'S FURNITURE. $5.00. Circle No. 71.

BATHROOMS, LAUNDRY, WATER SYSTEMS

72 **DELTA FAUCET COMPANY** — Designing durable, stylish products to complement any home. Receive our full-line catalogs. DELTA FAUCET COMPANY. Free. Circle No. 72.

73 **HANSA AMERICA** — For nearly a century, HANSA has been producing a wide array of faucets, accessories and bath and shower systems using fine German craftsmanship, creating bath settings that are truly Full of Life. HANSA AMERICA. Free. Circle No. 73.

74 **KWC FAUCETS** — Bringing Swiss quality faucets and accessories to the world for over 125 years, KWC has combined precision and function in sleek, stylish designs for the kitchen and bath. KWC FAUCETS, INC. Free. Circle No. 74.

75 **TOTO USA** — Send for a complete guide to TOTO high performance toilets, lavatories, and accessories. TOTO. $2.00. Circle No. 75.

KITCHEN PLANNING, EQUIPMENT, & APPLIANCES

76 **DACOR EPICURE APPLIANCES** — Commercial-style cooktops, ranges, and ovens offer superior performance and benefits including gas broiling in "Pure Convection™" self-cleaning electric ovens. DACOR. Free. Circle No. 76.

77 **DU PONT CORIAN®** — "Home as Self" from Corian® — a 20-page book filled with inspired Corian® applications and decorating philosophy, based on the idea that every home should fit its inhabitants. DU PONT CORIAN®. $2.00. Circle No. 77.

78 **GE** — Presenting cooking at the speed of life with the revolutionary Advantium Oven from GE. GENERAL ELECTRIC. Free. Circle No. 78.

79 **KOHLER BATH & KITCHEN IDEAS** — A complete set of full-color product catalogs covering baths and whirlpools, showers, lavatories, toilets and bidets, kitchen and entertainment sinks, faucets and accessories. KOHLER CO. $8.00. Circle No. 79.

80 **PLAIN & FANCY CUSTOM CABINETRY** — From American Arts & Crafts to the warmth of Provence, our new 40-page catalog previews these cabinetry styles and many more... and all within a price range you can afford. Available primarily east of the Mississippi. PLAIN & FANCY CUSTOM CABINETRY. $12.00. Circle No. 80.

81 **PRICE PFISTER** — The Pfreshest styles for your kitchen and bath. All products are backed by our Pforever Warranty covering the finish and function for life. PRICE PFISTER. Free. Circle No. 81.

82 **SIEMATIC** — The SieMatic Kitchen Book is 128 large-format pages full of exciting kitchen design ideas featuring SieMatic's internationally famous line of European and American style cabinets and accessories. SIEMATIC. $19.95. Circle No. 82.

83 **THERMADOR** — Learn why Thermador has become the brand of choice for so many cooking enthusiasts. Our color catalog offers you a wide range of options to meet your specific kitchen requirements. THERMADOR. Free. Circle No. 83.

84 **VIKING RANGE** — The originator of commercial-type equipment for the home, Viking Range outfits the ultimate kitchen with a full line of products. VIKING RANGE CORPORATION. Free. Circle No. 84.

85 **WEBER GRILLS** — For Savory recipes, expert grilling tips and information on the complete line of Weber® grills, send for a free brochure. WEBER-STEPHEN PRODUCTS CO. Free. Circle No. 85.

VARIOUS

86 **ACURA** — Get a closer look at the full line of Acura automobiles. Send for a complimentary brochure and information to find the showroom nearest you. ACURA. Free. Circle No. 86.

87 **CRANE STATIONERY** — Since 1801, Crane has made the finest in personal stationery, invitations, seasonal cards, and business papers. CRANE & CO. $5.00. Circle No. 87.

88 **DECORATING DEN INTERIORS** — Follow your dream, Interior Decorating! Build a great business and a beautiful career with the new Decorating Den Interiors. DECORATING DEN INTERIORS. Free. Circle No. 88.

89 **EBAY PREMIER** — Everything you know about premium auctions is about to change. Like a traditional setting, sellers guarantee their merchandise and buyers make their bids in complete confidence. EBAY PREMIER. Free. Circle No. 89.

90 **EDWARD R. HAMILTON BOOKSELLER** — Bargain books: Shop America's biggest selection, save up to 80%! Decorating, architecture, gardening, more. Quality hardcover books start at $3.95. Catalog. EDWARD R. HAMILTON BOOKSELLER. Free. Circle No. 90.

91 **FANCY FEAST GOURMET CAT FOOD** — For those who want only the best, there is Fancy Feast Gourmet Cat Food—exceptionally moist, uniquely delicious, and so many extraordinary varieties. Fancy Feast—Good taste is easy to recognize.™ FANCY FEAST GOURMET CAT FOOD. Free. Circle No. 91.

92 **NATIONAL FLOOD INSURANCE PROGRAM** — Be flood alert. Everyone lives in a flood zone. Fortunately you can protect your home and belongings with national flood insurance. Find out more today. Free information. FEMA. Free. Circle No. 92.

TABLEWARE

93 **LENOX® CHINA AND CRYSTAL** — If you are looking for the perfect gift for any occasion, "Lenox" is the place to go with unique gifts for any budget. Lenox: Gifts that Celebrate Life. LENOX, INC. Free. Circle No. 93.

OUTDOOR LIVING

94 **SUNBRELLA® FABRICS** — The Sunbrella® line of outdoor fabrics from Glen Raven Custom Fabrics offers a wide selection of styles designed for awnings, umbrellas and casual furniture. GLEN RAVEN CUSTOM FABRICS, L.L.C. Free. Circle No. 94.

95 **WHITE FLOWER FARM** — The foremost source of select ornamental plants, bulbs, and garden accessories. Send for a free catalogue. WHITE FLOWER FARM. Free. Circle No. 95.

PROPERTY

96 **DANIEL ISLAND, CHARLESTON, SC** — An island town blending neighborhoods, Fazio golf, parks, waterways, schools and business to live, work, play. DANIEL ISLAND REAL ESTATE. Free. Circle No. 96.

97 **KIAWAH ISLAND, SC** — Live along 10 miles of Atlantic beach, 45 miles of waterfront highland, and incomparable golf-front settings. KIAWAH ISLAND, SC. Free. Circle No. 97.

TRADITIONAL HOME

TRADITIONAL HOME®
JULY 2001
DEPT. TH0701IL
P.O. BOX 14430
DES MOINES, IA 50306-3430

NAME ______________________

ADDRESS ______________________

CITY ______________________

STATE/ZIP ______________________

PHONE NO. ______________________

I AM ENCLOSING:
$______________ TOTAL ENCLOSED

Are you planning to complete the following and if so, in which time frame? (circle all that apply)

Build:	0-3	3-6	6+ months
Remodel:	0-3	3-6	6+ months
Decorate:	0-3	3-6	6+ months
Add a room:	0-3	3-6	6+ months
Move:	0-3	3-6	6+ months

To Order By Phone Call Toll-Free
M–F: 7 a.m. to 11 p.m. Sat.: 8 a.m. to 4:30 p.m. CST:

1-800-547-0600

- Please have item numbers ready
- Credit Card purchases only

To Order By Mail:

- Circle your choice
- Complete Information Below
- Expired cards will not be processed

TO SUBSCRIBE TO TRADITIONAL HOME CIRCLE NO. 98
(1 Year U.S. $19.97.) Outside U.S. Circle No. 99 (1 year $25.97.)

1 .....Free	21 .....Free	41....$1.00	61....$5.00	81 .....Free
2 .....Free	22 .....Free	42....$5.00	62 .....Free	82..$19.95
3 .....Free	23 .....Free	43 .....Free	63....$3.00	83 .....Free
4....$1.00	24 .....Free	44 .....Free	64 .....Free	84 .....Free
5 .....Free	25....$3.00	45 .....Free	65 .....Free	85 .....Free
6..$16.00	26 .....Free	46 .....Free	66 .....Free	86 .....Free
7..$16.00	27 .....Free	47 .....Free	67 .....Free	87....$5.00
8....$2.00	28 .....Free	48 .....Free	68....$5.00	88 .....Free
9 .....Free	29 .....Free	49 .....Free	69 .....Free	89 .....Free
10....$7.00	30 .....Free	50....$2.00	70 .....Free	90 .....Free
11..$30.00	31 .....Free	51 .....Free	71....$5.00	91 .....Free
12 .....Free	32....$2.00	52 .....Free	72 .....Free	92 .....Free
13 .....Free	33..$20.00	53..$10.00	73 .....Free	93 .....Free
14 .....Free	34....$8.00	54..$25.00	74 .....Free	94 .....Free
15 .....Free	35 .....Free	55..$25.00	75....$2.00	95 .....Free
16 .....Free	36 .....Free	56 .....Free	76 .....Free	96 .....Free
17 .....Free	37....$2.00	57 .....Free	77....$2.00	97 .....Free
18 .....Free	38..$10.00	58 .....Free	78 .....Free	98..Bill me
19 .....Free	39 .....Free	59 .....Free	79....$8.00	99..Bill me
20 .....Free	40..$12.00	60 .....Free	80..$12.00	

Allow 6–8 weeks for delivery. Make checks payable to Traditional Home. Expiration Date: November 17, 2001

The Works

A Superb Mixture of Daffodils for Naturalizing

We call our Daffodil mixture The Works because it is carefully balanced among many different types of Daffodils to provide a long season of bloom with a full range of form and color. It consists of 100 top-quality bulbs of 40 excellent varieties. We're pleased to offer The Works for only $59 plus shipping (add sales tax to CT addresses). To order call **1-800-503-9624**, or order online at **www.whiteflowerfarm.com** and request item **984300**, or if you garden in the South, request item **984301** for our Southern mixture. Please reference code **12061** when ordering. The Works: **100 bulbs for $59, 200 for $99, 400 for $169.** Shipped for fall planting. Sincerely,

Amos Pettingill

White Flower Farm

PLANTSMEN SINCE 1950

LITCHFIELD, CT 06759-0050

Reader's Resource Continued from page 195
(Singburi/Pagoda #3046/10); **fabric on stacked
shades** (from the top, Songkla/Blue Harbor
#3047/07; Singburi/Magenta #3046/06;
Songkla/New Leaf #3047/03; Singburi/Paradise
Green #3046/18); **background fabric**
(Singburi/Dawn Mist #3046/13):
Jim Thompson Thai Silk, 800/262-0336, trade
Lampshade fabrication: Joyce Ames, Joyce
Ames Studio; 212/799-8995; by appointment c
Sofa: Akiko Busch's own. Similar available from
the new collection by Ralph Lauren (Renwick
Ralph Lauren Home, 800/578-7656.
Sofa fabric (Patong/Bangkok Grey #3054/14):
Thompson Thai Silk, 800/262-0336, trade only
Upholstery: Gary Buxbaum, 212/741-3899.
Second-hand **cherry dresser** lacquered kelly
green by TNT Woodworking, 37 W. 20th St., R
1204, New York, NY 10011; 212/255-6005.

PAGES 168–175
SMALL WONDERS
Model makers:
Mulvany & Rogers, 011 44 122 578 3611.
Studios of Harry Smith, Creating Fine Art Sinc
1959, 50 Harden Ave., Camden, ME 04843;
207/236-8162; fax 207/236-8169.

Where to see:
Tee Ridder Miniature Museum, 1 Museum D
Roslyn, Long Island; 516/484-7841.
The Toy & Miniature Museum of Kansas City,
5235 Oak St., on the University of Missouri-Ka
City campus; 816/333-9328.
The American Museum of Miniatures, Dallas,
214/969-5502.
The Thorne Rooms at the Art Institute of Chic
312/443-3600.

Miniature conventions: Sponsored by Tom
Bishop Productions, a miniaturists' show open
the public August 31 through September 2, at
Marriott Marquis in Manhattan. Artists from
around the world will display and sell tiny
furniture, paintings, silverware, needlework,
porcelain, and dolls. For more information, ca
954/755-0373.

PAGES 177–180
MENUS FOR GREAT GATHERINGS
GIRLFRIENDS' WEEKEND
Pages 177–180. **Black-and-white "Stripe"
pattern dinnerware** (dinner plate, $54; salad
dessert plate, $36; mug, $25): by Jonathan Adl
465 Broome St., New York, NY 10013; 212/941-
Yellow and white plates: Crate and Barrel,
800/237-5672.
Glassware (Festival Geometric highball): Pier
Imports, 800/447-4371; www.pier1.com.
Turquoise beaded place mat: by Kim Seybe
212/564-7850; www.kimseybert.com.
Square white plates with black design (Bo
Bonniere, by Chaleur; hand-painted bone chin
salad plates, $20): Exhome, 877/443-9466, for
store nearest you. ⊞ .

...OVERS BY

... Sure Fit

...ers allow you

...a love with

...rniture again.

...izes (chair,

..., soft) fit most

...ered furniture. Stylish, machine

...le fabrics like velvet, chenille, and damask. Pillows, recliner, dining

...d wing chair covers available. For a free catalog, call 1-888-SURE FIT

...787-3348) or visit our website at www.surefit.com.

WOOD CLASSICS

has a complete line of
beautiful, meticulously
crafted, teak outdoor
furniture, available
either fully assembled
or as precision cut kits.
Designed to last a life-

time, this maintenance-free furniture is ideal for any outdoor setting, in a
sunroom or on a screened porch. Call or write for our free catalog and
directions to our showroom, located just two hours north of New York
City. (845) 255-5651. WOOD CLASSICS, Box 101TH0411, Gardiner,
NY 12525. Shop online @ www.woodclassics.com.

Best Buys Now

A Selection of Special Values for Traditional Home Readers

FRAN'S WICKER
& RATTAN
FURNITURE –
Order with
confidence from
America's oldest and
largest wicker &
rattan importer.
Highest quality,
lower prices and

...delivery. For a Free 72-page catalog, call 800-531-1511 and ask
...t. TH01 or visit us at www.franswicker.com.

REJUVENATION LAMP &
FIXTURE CO. – See your home
in a better light – Rejuvenation
lighting. 280 authentic styles and
11 finishes, made to your order
and delivered to your door. Free
88-page catalogue. Call
888-3-GETLIT (888-343-8548)
or visit www.rejuvenation.com.

...SEASONS SUNROOMS

...NSERVATORIES –

...g 48 page catalog

...s America's largest

...n of sunrooms, English

...onservatories, patio rooms,

...res, hobby

...ouses and skylights.

...ve MC2 glass keeps out summer heat yet provides maximum

...on in winter. Available as a do-it-yourself kit or full installation

...ir Nationwide Dealer Network. Free color catalog. Call

...FOUR SEASONS (1-800-368-7732) or visit our website at

...ourseasonssunrooms.com/trh.

TIMBERLANE
WOODCRAFTERS, INC.
manufactures a full line of custom,
wood, exterior shutters. There are
over 21 unique styles and hundreds
of possible configurations to choose
from all built to your specifications.
Extensive selection of reproduction
shutter hardware kept in stock.
Call (800) 250-2221 for our free
64-page color catalog.
www.timberlanewoodcrafters.com.

How the gem of
Julius Caesar's eye
became a Victorian
badge of beauty

By Sam Haselby

CAMEO
APPEARANCE

Birth: Possibly a war baby. The cameo may have been carried across Asia to the Mediterranean world by Alexander the Great's army. Cameos first surfaced on the Nile Delta, in the great conqueror's namesake city, Alexandria, Egypt, circa 330 B.C.

Ancestry: Unlike the incised intaglio, cameos stand out in relief. The stone's outstanding sculptural qualities appealed to powerful potentates and helped launch the cameo's centuries-long career as the jewelry of emperors.

The most famous cameo, the Gemma Augustea, commemorated the Roman Emperor Augustus and dates from the first century A.D. The exquisite, carved-onyx portrait of Augustus as Jupiter was inspired not only by Alexander the Great's collection but by that of another emperor, Augustus's adopted uncle, Julius Caesar, who collected cameos to offer to the temple of Venus. Napoleon, who in the early 19th century positioned himself as the inheritor of the reigns of Caesar and Augustus, copied their taste in jewelry as well. The *Couronne de Sacre*, Napoleon's gold-plated coronation crown, is studded with dozens of antique Roman cameos. Napoleon even established a school in Paris that specialized in carving cameos.

Thomas Jefferson, an empire builder on the other side of Atlantic, set blue-and-white Wedgwood Jasperware cameos Monticello's fireplace mantel.

Lineage: Catherine the Great was one of the cameo's first wo champions. The Russian empress owned over 32,000 of t When the connoisseur couldn't get her hands on antique gems ordered hundreds of glass-paste imitations from Scottish scu James Tassie. Today, Catherine's vast cameo collection ca found in the Hermitage museum in St. Petersburg.

Like Alexander, Caesar, Augustus, Catherine, and Napo Queen Victoria was a cameo collector. Simply by wearing favorites, cameos carved from shells, Victoria transformed medallion of monarchs into a badge of beauty and femininity

Why They Still Work: Whether wrapped around the nec perched above a plunging neckline, cameos are like a bea bow on a gift-wrapped package, a hymn to the décolle Perhaps that's why Gillian Anderson wore a cameo choke her role as socialite Lily Bart in Terence Davies' recent *House of Mirth*. 🏛

ALL-NEW ENVOY
EXCEPTIONAL COMFORT

TOM SUTTER WANTS YOU TO FEEL RELAXED.
NOT FALL ASLEEP.

INTRODUCING THE ALL-NEW GMC ENVOY.
THE NEXT GENERATION OF SUVs.

COMFORT

EXCEPTIONALLY SMOOTH RIDE.	BEFORE YOU IS THE FIRST MID-SIZE SUV TO USE HYDROFORMED STEEL TECHNOLOGY. THIS INNOVATIVE METHOD PLUS BILSTEIN® SHOCKS, AN ADVANCED SUSPENSION SYSTEM AND EXCLUSIVELY DESIGNED MICHELIN® TIRES CREATE A PHENOMENAL RIDE, VIRTUALLY FREE OF NOISE AND VIBRATION ON ALMOST ANY ROAD SURFACE.
270 HP VORTEC™ 4200.	TOM AND THE ENGINEERING TEAM GAVE ENVOY AN ENGINE WITH MORE HORSEPOWER THAN ANY OTHER MID-SIZE SUV IN ITS CLASS, EVEN THOSE WITH V8 ENGINES* MERGE INTO TRAFFIC AND THIS QUIET ENGINE KICKS INTO STUNNING EXHILARATION.

**TOM SUTTER
POWERTRAIN
ENGINEER**

TOM'S CREDO: COMFORT
AND INVIGORATION
GO HAND IN HAND.

1 888- ENVOY4U OR GMC.COM/ENVOY

FROM PROFESSIONAL GRADE PEOPLE
COME PROFESSIONAL GRADE SUVS. | WE ARE PROFESSIONAL GRADE.™

SOPRANO RENÉE FLEMING.
A VOICE SO BEAUTIFUL IT CAN BREAK YOUR HEART.

When critics try to capture the special quality of Renée Fleming, they focus on the moving humanity of her performance. Perhaps that's why she's chosen a timepiece that for all its beauty is strong enough to be enjoyed in the real world.

ROLEX

Rolex Lady-Datejust in 18kt gold. Enlarged for detail.